THE ACADEMY COLLECTION
QUICK REFERENCE GUIDES FOR FAMILY PHYSICIANS

OFFICE
PROCEDURE
FORMS

THE ACADEMY COLLECTION
QUICK REFERENCE GUIDES FOR FAMILY PHYSICIANS

OFFICE PROCEDURE FORMS

THOMAS J. ZUBER, MD
Program Director in Family Medicine
Saginaw Cooperative Hospitals
Saginaw, Michigan
Associate Professor
Michigan State University

Series Medical Editor
RICHARD SADOVSKY, MD, MS
Associate Professor of Family Medicine
State University of New York Health Science Center
Brooklyn, New York

Williams & Wilkins
A WAVERLY COMPANY
BALTIMORE • PHILADELPHIA • LONDON • PARIS • BANGKOK
BUENOS AIRES • HONG KONG • MUNICH • SYDNEY • TOKYO • WROCLAW

Editor: Jonathan W. Pine, Jr
Managing Editor: Molly L. Mullen
Development Editor: Robert Newman, Co Medica, Inc.
AAFP Project Manager: Leigh McKinney
Marketing Manager: Daniell Griffin
Project Editor: Paula C. Williams
Design Coordinator: Mario Fernandez

351 West Camden Street
Baltimore, Maryland 21201-2436 USA

Rose Tree Corporate Center
1400 North Providence Road
Building II, Suite 5025
Media, Pennsylvania 19063-2043 USA

Printed in the United States of America

Library of Congress Cataloging-in-Publication Data

Zuber, Thomas J.
Office procedure forms / Thomas J. Zuber.
p. cm.—(The Academy collection—quick reference guides for family physicians)
Includes index.
ISBN 0-683-30580-8
1. Medical records—Forms. 2. Medical history taking—Forms. 3. Informed consent (Medical law)—Forms. 4. Nursing records—Forms. I. Title. II. Series.
[DNLM: 1. Ambulatory Surgical Procedures. 2. Patient Education. 3. Informed Consent forms. 4. Medical History Taking forms. 5. Nursing Records forms. WO 192 Z93oa 1998]
R864.Z83 1998
651.5′04261—dc21
DNLM/DLC
for Library of Congress 98-23693
CIP

99 00 01 02
1 2 3 4 5 6 7 8 9 10

This book has required many long hours for completion. I want to dedicate it to those who sacrificed so much for its completion: Julie, Laura, TJ, and Andrew. I also acknowledge the encouragement of those physicians who have fought for the place of procedures in family medicine.

Thomas J. Zuber

SERIES INTRODUCTION

Family practice is a unique clinical specialty encompassing a philosophy of care rather than a modality of care provided to a specific segment of the population. This philosophy of providing longitudinal care for persons of all ages in the complete context of their physical, emotional, and social environments was modeled by general practitioners, the parents of our modern specialty. To provide this kind of care, the family physician needs a broad knowledge base, appropriate evaluation tools, effective interventions, and patient education.

The knowledge base needed by a family physician is extraordinarily large. The American Academy of Family Physicians and other organizations provide clinical education through conferences and journals. Individual family physicians have written journal articles about a specific clinical topic or have tried to cover the broad knowledge base of family medicine in a single volume. The former are helpful, but may cover only a narrow segment of medicine, while the latter may not provide the depth needed to be useful in actual patient care.

The Academy Collection: Quick Reference Guides for Family Physicians is a series of books designed to assist family physicians with the broad knowledge base unique to our specialty. The books in this series have all been written by practicing family physicians who have special interest in the topics, and the chapters have been formatted to provide easy access to information needed at varying stages in the physician–patient encounter. Each volume is unique because each author has personalized the volume and provided a unique family physician perspective.

This series is not meant to be a final reference for the family physician who seeks a comprehensive text. The series also does not cover every topic that may be encountered by the family physician. The series does offer, in a depth determined appropriate by the authors, the information needed by the physician to handle the majority of patient encounters. The series also provides information to make patient care a combined doctor–patient effort. Specific patient education materials have been included where appropriate. Readers can contact the American Academy of Family Physicians Foundation for other resources.

The topics selected for the *Academy Collection* were chosen based on what family physicians said they needed. The first group of books covers office procedures, conditions of aging, and some of the most challenging diagnoses seen in family practice. Future books in the series will address musculoskeletal problems, occupational/environmental medicine, children's health, skin conditions, and gastrointestinal problems.

I welcome your comments. Please contact me at the American Academy of Family Physicians with your suggestions (Rick Sadovsky, M.D., Series Editor, The Academy Collection, c/o AAFP, 8880 Ward Parkway, Kansas City, MO 64116; e-mail: academycollection@aafp.org). This collection is meant to be useful to you and your patients.

Richard Sadovsky, M.D., M.S.
Series Editor

CONTENTS

INTRODUCTION

Procedural services provide diagnostic or therapeutic interventions for patients that can result in improved health. The proper performance of office procedural services includes more than just the technical manual skills. Physicians have a responsibility to provide patients with sufficient knowledge to decide to undergo an intervention that often places patients at some risk. To assist with the process of providing informed consent, each chapter in this book includes an informed consent form that lists the risks and complications specific to a particular procedure.

Offices that provide procedural services must also inform patients of the necessary preparation and recovery instructions for any service they perform. Preprocedure and postprocedure information sheets have been designed to assist in this process. There is a substantial body of medical literature that suggests that patient education assists in patient comfort during a procedure. Our practice distributes or mails these education forms whenever a patient is scheduled into the procedures clinics.

When training physicians to perform procedural services, it is helpful to provide prompts or reminders for each of the steps in a particular sequence. Procedure documentation forms can serve to remind the physician, while also avoiding the expensive transcription costs associated with a lengthy procedure. Insurance companies now require proper documentation of a procedure to allow for reimbursement. The procedure documentation forms included in this book should meet all of these objectives.

Nursing staffs need instructions for the proper set-up and cleaning of equipment involved in a particular procedure. Nursing checklists can aid in the smooth performance of any procedure. The nursing instruction sheets included in this book also provide patient care instructions for the immediate preprocedure and postprocedure periods.

This book represents a compilation of office procedure forms and is designed to meet the needs of both the provider and patient. Each chapter includes a preprocedure patient instruction sheet, a postprocedure instruction sheet, an informed consent form, a nursing sheet, and a procedure documentation form. The first three sheets are distributed to patients before the procedure, and the last two sheets are used by the clinic on the day of the procedure. The nursing instruction sheets are kept in a notebook for ease of accessibility. Practices may wish to add their letterhead or logo to the top of these forms when copying them for use.

Informed consent laws vary from state to state. Physicians are encouraged to learn their state's individual rules. While the informed consent forms included in this book provide some elements of informed consent, physicians are encouraged to obtain verbal consent before any procedure. No written form can provide complete liability protection.

Other forms have been added to certain chapters to provide useful information needed for the performance of specific procedures. For instance, the flexible sigmoidoscopy chapter has an added sheet on cleaning and disinfecting the sigmoidoscope. The esophagogastroduodenoscopy chapter includes a nursing flowsheet/checklist to assist with the extensive nursing duties during that procedure.

These forms are designed to complement the information in the companion book, *Office Procedures*, in *The Academy Collection: Quick Reference Guides for Family Physicians* series. This book includes information on procedure pitfalls and complications, follow-up of procedure findings, equipment ordering information, and coding and reimbursement for the specific procedure.

Thomas J. Zuber, M.D.

SECTION I

DIAGNOSTIC PROCEDURES

CHAPTER 1

Colposcopy

PATIENT INFORMATION

Colposcopy

What is colposcopy?

Colposcopy is the examination of a woman's cervix and genital tissues with a special microscope called a colposcope. Colposcopy can be done after an abnormal Pap smear to examine for abnormal growths or to rule out cancer. The Pap smear is a good screening test for disease but results can be incorrect up to 30% of the time. Colposcopy can predict more accurately the extent of disease on the cervix.

How is the procedure performed?

Your doctor will explain the procedure to you. Your legs then will be placed in stirrups (just like when you have a Pap smear). After the speculum is placed in the vagina, vinegar is applied to the cervix. The vinegar can cause some brief, mild burning. Abnormal tissue turns white with the vinegar and can be seen with the colposcope. If the tissue appears abnormal, the doctor will perform a scraping and biopsies. The scraping excludes disease in the canal of the cervix and only takes about 15 seconds. If biopsies, or little pieces of tissue, are to be removed from the outside of the cervix, the doctor may spray some numbing medicine first. The biopsies take just a few seconds, and then some brown iron solution is applied to the cervix to stop any bleeding.

How should I prepare for colposcopy?

You can take ibuprofen (brand names: Advil, Motrin, Nuprin), four 200-mg tablets with food, about 1 hour before coming to the office. The ibuprofen reduces the uterine cramping that can occur with the procedure. You may be asked to complete some paperwork just before the procedure. The entire visit takes 30 to 40 minutes, and you should be able to drive home immediately following the procedure.

Will my cervix be treated at the time of the colposcopy?

Some doctors choose to treat the cervix based on the appearance of the cervix through the colposcope; however, this can result in the overtreatment of many women. A more appropriate and cost-effective approach is to treat women based on the biopsy results obtained at colposcopy. The small pieces of tissue removed during the colposcopy procedure are examined at the hospital by a specialist physician called a pathologist. It takes about a week to get the biopsy results, and your doctor's office will contact you when the results are available. If you require additional treatment, such as removal of extensive diseased tissue of the cervix, that can be performed in 1 month during the follow-up visit. Because some mild changes to the cervix can be monitored without a surgical procedure, your doctor will want to talk to you in 1 month. Please return for that follow-up visit to be sure you understand the treatment plan that is best for you.

This handout provides a general overview on this subject and may not apply to everyone. Talk to your family doctor to find out if this information applies to you and to get more information.

PATIENT INFORMATION

HPV and Cervical Dysplasia

What is HPV?

HPV, or human papillomavirus, is a common infection in people. There are more than 60 types of HPV viruses. HPV has been called the wart virus. Types 1, 3, and 5 commonly cause warts on the hands and feet of children. Types 6 and 11 cause genital warts. Other types, such as 16 and 18, may not cause warts but can cause precancerous or cancerous changes to the cells of the cervix or vagina.

What is cervical dysplasia?

Cervical dysplasia is a precancerous change to the cells at the base of the uterus (womb). Although cervical dysplasia is caused by many factors, including cigarette smoking, HPV infection has been associated with most cases of dysplasia. There are three types of dysplasia: mild, moderate, and severe. Mild dysplasia is the most common, and probably is not a true precancerous change but is the body's response to HPV infection. In up to 70% of women with mild dysplasia, the changes resolve without treatment. Moderate and severe dysplasia require treatment because they change into cancer more often.

How can I tell if I have HPV?

Most people with HPV never know they have the virus. Only one person in 100 with the virus will have warts. The infection is very common, and nearly one-quarter of all sexually active individuals under age 30 probably carry the virus. A Pap smear can often detect HPV. Even if changes from HPV are not detected by the Pap smear, you can be 80 to 90% certain that the virus is present if cervical dysplasia is detected.

How did I get HPV?

Most people get genital HPV through sexual contact. Condoms can prevent the spread of many diseases but they do not completely prevent the transmission of HPV. People can get the virus as teenagers, but have no signs of the virus for up to 20 years. This may explain why a woman suddenly develops warts or dysplasia after many years of sexual inactivity. A woman who has a first abnormal Pap smear may or may not have just acquired HPV.

Can I get rid of HPV and dysplasia?

Cervical dysplasia can be eliminated by many surgical techniques. However, the virus often remains on the cervix, even following extensive burning or lasering of the cervical tissues. The goal of treatment is not the elimination of the virus, but for the body's immune system to control the HPV infection. Immune system function can be enhanced by not smoking and, possibly, by taking antioxidant vitamins. Your doctor will talk to you about the treatment options for cervical dysplasia, depending on the degree (grade) of dysplasia that is detected.

This handout provides a general overview on this subject and may not apply to everyone. Talk to your family doctor to find out if this information applies to you and to get more information.

PATIENT INSTRUCTIONS

Following Colposcopy

1. You may have some cramping or discomfort following the procedure. You can take ibuprofen (brand names: Advil, Motrin, Nuprin), three 200-mg tablets three times a day with food. Most women return to work several hours later, or the day after the procedure.

2. A brownish iron solution (called Monsel's paste) was applied to your cervix to control any bleeding during the procedure. You may want to place an absorbent pad in your underwear to prevent staining. Please do not place a tampon in the vagina. Brownish drainage usually continues for several days after the procedure.

3. Please do not have sex (intercourse) for 2 to 3 weeks following the procedure. Do not place anything in the vagina during this time. Women often develop bleeding or spotting if they resume intercourse too early.

4. Infection is very uncommon following colposcopy. Call your doctor's office if you have any fever, foul-smelling discharge, or heavy bleeding in the first few days following the procedure.

5. Women can improve the body's ability to fight the virus (HPV) that causes most cervical dysplasia. The body's immune system can better control the virus if the woman does not smoke and does not have nutritional deficiencies. Some experts recommend a daily multivitamin to enhance the ability to control HPV. Smokers should quit smoking.

6. It takes about 1 week to get the results of the biopsy specimens taken during colposcopy. Your doctor's office will contact you once the results are available.

7. The need for further treatment is determined by the results of the biopsies. Low-grade changes can sometimes be monitored closely, but high-grade changes almost always require some type of surgical treatment. Your doctor will discuss these treatment options with you at the follow-up visit in 1 month.

8. Please return to the office in 1 month. Even if no treatment is planned at that time, the visit is important to talk about the planned follow-up for the next year. Women can develop cancer following a normal colposcopy, and you should keep scheduled follow-up visits.

This handout provides a general overview on this subject and may not apply to everyone. Talk to your family doctor to find out if this information applies to you and to get more information.

INFORMED CONSENT FORM

Colposcopy

PATIENT: ______________________________

DATE: ____________________

1. I hereby authorize Dr. ________________ to perform the procedure known as colposcopy.

2. I understand that colposcopy is performed to examine the cervix and genital tract with a special microscope called a colposcope. This procedure is commonly performed to evaluate an abnormal Pap smear, or to exclude the presence of cancer of the cervix. I understand that the Pap smear is a screening test, and that the biopsies obtained at colposcopy more accurately reflect the extent of disease on the cervix. I understand that the scraping and biopsies that are performed can cause some cramping and discomfort. I understand that the practice of medicine is not an exact science, and that no guarantee can be made regarding the outcome of my planned procedure.

3. My doctor has explained to me that this procedure is generally safe, but that certain risks accompany any surgical procedure. Risks associated with colposcopy include:

   Bleeding during the procedure or in the days following

   Pain associated with the procedure or in the hours following

   Allergic reaction to the numbing medication or the surgical instruments

   Infection in the genital tract or uterus

   Dizziness or passing out

   Rare, unusual reactions, including possible death following any surgical procedure

4. I understand that there are alternative diagnostic procedures that could be performed, including surgical removal of tissue to analyze the cells of the cervix. I understand that I can refuse this procedure.

5. I understand that unforeseen conditions may alter the planned procedure. I give permission to my doctor to alter the procedure (such as to perform electrocautery or to suture a bleeding biopsy site), if necessary, or to administer additional anesthetics or other medications if I should need them for the completion of my procedure.

6. I have read this form and other sheets given to me by my physician. I have had my questions answered to my satisfaction.

WITNESS: ____________________

PATIENT: ____________________

DATE: ____________________

MINOR: ____________________

PARENT: ____________________

NURSING INSTRUCTIONS

Colposcopy

PREPROCEDURE INSTRUCTIONS

Ask the patient if she took her preprocedure ibuprofen (Motrin). If not, offer her four 200-mg ibuprofen tablets and a glass of water.

Ask the patient to undress from the waist down. A sheet is given to the patient to cover her waist and legs. The patient is seated on the examination table to talk with the physician.

The colposcope is plugged in and positioned near the bottom of the table.

NONSTERILE TRAY FOR THE PROCEDURE

Place the following items on a nonsterile sheet covering a Mayo stand:

Nonsterile Graves' large vaginal speculum

12 large cotton-tipped swabs

12 small cotton-tipped swabs

2 labeled formalin specimen containers

Acetic acid (vinegar) in a small plastic medicine cup

Monsel's paste in a small plastic medicine cup

Ring (Foerster) forceps

Tischler cervical biopsy forceps instrument

Endocervical curette (without basket)

Endocervical speculum (if desired)

Wooden toothpicks (for removing biopsy specimens from biopsy instrument)

Cut piece of Telfa pad (1/2 inch × 1/2 inch)

Absorbent external pad (to place in the patient's underwear after the procedure)

INSTRUCTIONS FOLLOWING THE PROCEDURE

Remove all instruments and materials from the tray at the base of the examination table. Assist the patient to a seated position and give the patient an absorbent pad for her underwear.

Ask the patient to get dressed for her postprocedure conference with the physician. Staff can leave the room to provide the patient additional privacy.

The specimen containers and pathology request forms should be labeled and completed. Make sure the patient's phone number is available on the chart to notify her of the biopsy results.

Soiled or bloodied swabs and materials are disposed of in an appropriate biohazard waste container.

The instruments are washed and steam sterilized in the autoclave.

PROCEDURE RECORDING FORM

Colposcopy

PATIENT NAME: ______________________________

DATE: ______________

AGE: ______________

Circle the Correct Response:

Smoker?	Yes	No	History of cervical cryosurgery?	Yes	No
History of genital warts?	Yes	No	History of LEEP / Laser surgery?	Yes	No
History of AIDS?	Yes	No	History of immunodeficiency?	Yes	No

Prior treatment of the cervix (include year): ______________________________
Date of most recent Pap smear: ______________________________
Result: ______________________________
Indications for colposcopy: ______________________________

External Genitalia

FR - Friability
ER - Erosion
LK - Leukoplakia
MA - Mild Acetowhite
DA - Dense Acetowhite
PN - Punctation
MO - Mosaic
FN - Fine
CO - Coarse
AV - Atypical Vessels
X - Biopsy Sites
W - Wart
SCJ - SquamoCol. Jnct
OS - Cervical Os

Cervical Examination

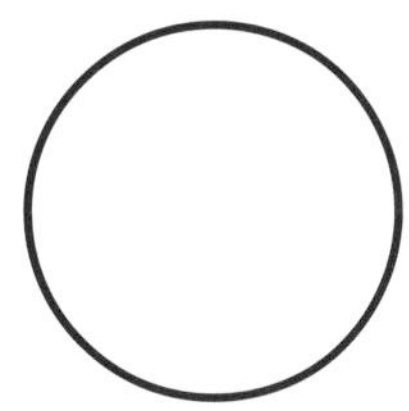

Cytology: Yes No ECC: Yes No
Ext. Biopsy, site: ______________________________
Cervical Biopsy sites: ______________________________
Impression:

_____ Abnormal colposcopic appearance
_____ Adequate colposcopy
_____ Abnormal cervical growths
_____ Abnormal external lesions

Plan:

_____ Patient and partner discouraged from smoking
_____ Follow-up in 1 month; further therapy pending the biopsy results
_____ Patient counseled in importance of follow-up, repeat Pap smears
_____ Patient aware of need for surgical intervention if HSIL on biopsy
_____ Patient aware of monitoring option for LSIL

Postprocedure instruction sheet given.

Physician: ______________
CC: ______________

CHAPTER 2

Endometrial Biopsy

PATIENT INFORMATION

Endometrial Biopsy

What is endometrial biopsy?

Endometrial biopsy is a safe and effective method for evaluating the tissue lining the inside of the uterus (or womb). A plastic catheter is slipped into the uterus, and a small amount of the endometrial lining is suctioned into the catheter. This technique has been demonstrated to provide a tissue sample equal to or superior to the older dilatation and curettage (D&C) procedure.

Why is endometrial biopsy performed?

Endometrial biopsy is performed to evaluate the uterus lining for the presence of cancer or precancerous cells. Most women who have this procedure done have abnormal uterine bleeding, or prolonged absence of their periods (amenorrhea). Other women who undergo this procedure include those on hormones (taking estrogen but not progesterone) or those at high risk for endometrial cancer (hereditary nonpolyposis colorectal cancer).

Is endometrial biopsy painful?

It can be uncomfortable. The placement of the thin plastic catheter inside the uterus can produce cramping. Take four 200-mg ibuprofen tablets with some food about an hour before coming to the office for the procedure. To reduce the discomfort from instruments used during the procedure, the cervix can be sprayed with a numbing medicine. The numbing spray may sting for a few seconds. The entire procedure takes just a few minutes, and most women tolerate the procedure well.

What complications may develop after endometrial biopsy?

You may experience vaginal bleeding for days following the procedure. If you are pregnant at the time of the procedure, the pregnancy can be damaged, so before the procedure tell your doctor if there is a possibility that you are pregnant. Some women may develop infection in the uterus or fallopian tubes any time an instrument is placed into the uterus, but this is very rare following endometrial biopsy. Rarely, a hole can be made in the wall of the uterus by the thin plastic catheter, especially if the uterus is angled up or down.

What happens to the sample that is removed from the lining of my uterus?

The sample is sent to the hospital for examination by a specialist physician called a pathologist. The cells from the tissue are examined under the microscope, and the pathologist can determine if cancerous or precancerous cells are present. Your doctor's office will contact you once the report of the tissue examination is completed.

This handout provides a general overview on this subject and may not apply to everyone. Talk to your family doctor to find out if this information applies to you and to get more information.

PATIENT INSTRUCTIONS

Following Endometrial Biopsy

1. If you have any discomfort after the procedure, you may take ibuprofen (brand names: Advil, Motrin, Nuprin), three 200-mg tablets three times a day with food. Acetaminophen (brand name: Tylenol) can also be taken, but is not as effective in reducing the uterine cramping.

2. You may drive home following the procedure, unless additional medications have to be given in the office to complete your procedure.

3. Some vaginal bleeding or spotting is common following the procedure. If you experience heavy bleeding, please call your doctor.

4. Infection following the procedure is uncommon, but report any complaints that would suggest an infection, such as pain in the lower abdomen or vagina or a foul-smelling vaginal discharge. Your doctor may prescribe an antibiotic for a few days following the procedure to prevent infection.

5. Please do not place anything in your vagina, and avoid sex (intercourse) for 1 week following the procedure.

6. A nurse will call you with the report of the tests done on the tissue removed from your uterus. You may be asked to take hormones if abnormal cells are detected. Your doctor will talk to you about the best treatment strategy for you when you return to the office for a follow-up visit in a few weeks.

This handout provides a general overview on this subject and may not apply to everyone. Talk to your family doctor to find out if this information applies to you and to get more information.

INFORMED CONSENT FORM

Endometrial Biopsy

PATIENT: ______________________________

DATE: __________________

1. I hereby authorize Dr. ______________ to perform the procedure known as endometrial biopsy.

2. I understand that this is a procedure performed to evaluate the tissue lining the inside of my uterus (womb). The procedure is usually performed to evaluate abnormal or excessive vaginal bleeding, lack of vaginal bleeding, or to exclude the presence of cancer. A thin plastic catheter is inserted into my uterus, and moved back and forth as suction is applied to obtain a tissue sample. The physician may need to dilate the opening to my uterus to pass the catheter into the womb. The entire procedure can be somewhat uncomfortable, and efforts will be made to minimize my discomfort. I understand that the practice of medicine is not an exact science, and that no guarantee can be made regarding the outcome of my planned procedure.

3. My doctor has explained to me that the procedure is generally safe, but that certain risks accompany any procedure. Risks associated with endometrial biopsy include:

Bleeding, sometimes lasting for several days after the procedure

Damage to an unknown pregnancy that is present when the biopsy is performed

Pain and cramping

Perforation (a hole in the uterus wall) that may require surgical closure

Allergic reaction to medications or instruments used

Infection in the uterus or nearby tissues

Rare, unusual reactions, including possible death following any surgical procedure

4. I understand that there are alternatives to this procedure, such as visualizing the uterine lining with hysteroscopy, ultrasound, or CT scan. I understand that the alternate procedures are more expensive, and may not provide information beyond what endometrial biopsy can provide. I understand that I can refuse the procedure.

5. I understand that unforeseen conditions may alter the planned procedure. I give permission to my doctor to alter the procedure (such as to mechanically dilate a closed cervical canal), if necessary, or to administer additional anesthetics or medications if I should need them for the completion of my procedure.

6. I have read this form and other sheets given to me by my physician. I have had my questions answered to my satisfaction.

WITNESS: __________________ **PATIENT:** __________________

DATE: __________________

MINOR: __________________

PARENT: __________________

NURSING INSTRUCTIONS

Endometrial Biopsy

NONSTERILE TRAY: EXAMINATION FOR UTERINE POSITION

Nonsterile gloves

Lubricating jelly

Absorbent pad placed beneath the patient on the examination table

Formalin container (for endometrial sample) with the patient's name and the date recorded on the label

20% benzocaine (Hurricaine) spray with extended application nozzle

STERILE TRAY FOR THE PROCEDURE

Place the following items on a sterile drape covering the Mayo stand:

Sterile gloves

Sterile vaginal speculum

Uterine sound

Sterile metal basin with cotton balls and povidone-iodine inside

Endometrial suction catheter

Cervical tenaculum

Ring forceps (for wiping the cervix with the cotton balls)

Sterile 4 × 4 gauze (to wipe off gloves or equipment)

Sterile scissors (if the physician chooses to cut off the catheter tip to deliver the endometrial sample into the formalin container)

Keep sterile cervical dilators available, but do not open the sterile packaging unless the dilators are needed.

Nurse can spray the benzocaine spray onto the cervix for 5 seconds, avoiding contamination of the sterile speculum with the extended nozzle, once the physician is sterile-gloved and has placed the speculum.

POSTPROCEDURE NURSING INSTRUCTIONS

Assist the patient off the examination table, and offer the patient an absorbent pad to place in the underwear for any procedure-related drainage or bleeding.

Offer the patient ibuprofen (Motrin) if the patient did not take any preprocedure medication.

Fill out the pathology forms and send the sample to the laboratory.

The instruments should be scrubbed, washed, rinsed, and dried. Place the instruments in a clear sterilization packet, either individually or as a surgical tray, and sterilize in the autoclave.

Bloody or soiled gauze, cotton balls, and the catheter should be disposed of in an appropriate biohazard waste container.

PROCEDURE RECORDING FORM

Endometrial Biopsy

PATIENT NAME: ______________________________

DATE: ______________

AGE: ______________

How long symptoms have been present: ______________________

Circle the Correct Response:

Abnormal uterine bleeding?	Yes	No
Amenorrhea?	Yes	No
Prior endometrial hyperplasia?	Yes	No
Hereditary nonpolyposis colon Ca?	Yes	No
Prior AGUS Pap smear?	Yes	No
Obesity?	Yes	No
Diabetes mellitus?	Yes	No
HIV positive?	Yes	No
Unopposed estrogen therapy?	Yes	No

Date of last Pap smear: ______________

Finding: ______________

Date of last endometrial biopsy: ______________

Finding: ______________

Date of last menstrual period: ______________

Pregnancy test prior to procedure? Yes No

Preprocedure bimanual examination revealed the uterus position: ______________

Procedure Description: The patient gave informed consent for the procedure. The patient took, or was offered, preprocedure ibuprofen. The patient was placed in the lithotomy position and bimanual examination was performed to check the uterine position and uterocervical angle. The sterile speculum was inserted and the cervix was centered in the speculum. The cervix was sprayed for 5 seconds with 20% benzocaine solution. Sterile gloves were placed and the cervix was cleansed with povidone-iodine solution. An attempt was made to insert the uterine sound, but the cervix was mobile and required stabilization with a tenaculum placed on the anterior lip of the cervix. The sound was then placed to the fundus. The endometrial catheter was placed to the fundus, suction was created by withdrawing the piston, and multiple passes were made in the endometrial cavity while the catheter was twirled or spun. The catheter was then removed and the endometrial sample placed in formalin. The tenaculum was removed, hemostasis was confirmed, the vagina was swabbed clear of blood, and the speculum was removed. The patient tolerated the procedure well.

Uterine sound omitted?	Yes	No
Tenaculum placement omitted?	Yes	No
Second pass made with endometrial catheter?	Yes	No
Cervix dilated with Pratt dilators?	Yes	No

Complications: ______________________

Postprocedure antibiotic given? Yes _____ No _____

Diagnosis: ______________________

Plan: ______________________

Physician: ______________________

CC: ______________________

CHAPTER 3

Esophagogastroduodenoscopy

PATIENT INFORMATION

Gastroesophageal Reflux

What is gastroesophageal reflux?

Gastroesophageal reflux is the flow of stomach contents and acid back into the esophagus (swallowing tube). Some people may experience small amounts of reflux each day. People with gastroesophageal reflux disease (GERD) have greater amounts of stomach contents that pass upward, and they experience more frequent and excessive episodes of reflux. People who are overweight or who have a "beer belly" more commonly have GERD.

What are the symptoms of gerd?

Heartburn (called pyrosis) is the most common symptom. Heartburn is generally described as a burning sensation in the center of the chest. If the acid backflows all the way to your throat, you may experience increased saliva production, hoarseness, a foul taste or even ear infections. Acid reflux can produce chest pain, wheezing or tightness in the chest, or hiccups.

What foods or activities make the reflux worse?

Several foods or activities can relax the muscle at the top of the stomach and allow the acid to flow upward. Alcoholic beverages, smoking, chocolate, peppermint, and caffeine can all increase heartburn and reflux. Certain acid-containing foods, such as tomatoes, oranges, or citrus drinks, can also make symptoms worse. Eating large meals, eating before bed, eating before vigorous exercise, lying down, or bending over can all cause reflux.

Do any medicines make reflux worse?

Many medicines can relax the muscle at the top of the stomach and make reflux worse. Theophylline, an asthma medicine, relaxes the muscle and the resulting reflux can increase wheezing and asthma symptoms. Other medicines, such as calcium channel blockers used for high blood pressure or heart disease, the anxiety medication Valium, or certain medicines for depression, can worsen GERD.

What can I do to reduce my symptoms of reflux?

Losing weight, wearing loosely fitting clothes, avoiding night-time snacks, and avoiding offending foods can help to reduce episodes of reflux. Also avoid running or exercising right after eating. Raise the head of your bed to help keep acid in the stomach at night (the top bedposts can be placed inside large coffee cans filled with sand). Spouses often dislike the elevation in the first 2 weeks, but eventually adjust to the bed angle. You can tightly tuck in the bed sheets, and slide under the sheets from above to help reduce the tendency to slide down during the night.

This handout provides a general overview on this subject and may not apply to everyone. Talk to your family doctor to find out if this information applies to you and to get more information.

PATIENT INFORMATION

Esophagogastroduodenoscopy (EGD)

What is esophagogastroduodenoscopy?

Also called EGD, this procedure uses a flexible, lighted tube to examine your esophagus (swallowing tube), stomach, and duodenum (first portion of your small bowel). The exam can be performed in the office, and it provides an accurate way to diagnose problems in your upper gastrointestinal tract. EGD often is used to diagnose ulcers, but it is a valuable aid to your doctor in the evaluation of many upper abdomen or chest complaints.

Is the procedure uncomfortable?

Some people become anxious during EGD or experience mild discomfort. Your doctor will give you medicines to help you relax. Historically, medicines were given intravenously (through an IV tube). However, an alternate regimen is for you to take two Halcion tablets by mouth before leaving home to come to the office for the procedure. Before the procedure, we may administer medicine in a nasal spray for further relaxation. We do not want you unconscious for the procedure, because you need to swallow during the procedure. Several medicines also will be given to numb your throat.

Will I be attached to any monitors during the procedure?

For added safety, your heart and breathing will be monitored. Several small sticky electrodes will be placed on your skin to monitor your heart. A small clip is placed over your finger to monitor the amount of oxygen in your blood. Your blood pressure also is watched closely during the procedure.

How is the exam performed?

You will be lying on a table on your left side for the EGD examination. A small plastic block is placed between your teeth, and the scope is inserted through this block. A thin scope is used for added comfort and safety. To get the scope into your esophagus, you will be asked to swallow. To check for a hiatal hernia, you may be asked to sniff. Most people rest or sleep for the rest of the examination, and tolerate it well. Your doctor will talk with you and someone with you (family member or friend) after the procedure. The actual examination takes about 30 minutes, but plan on being at the office for about 1 ½ hours.

What do I need to do before the exam?

Your stomach must be empty, so please do not eat anything after midnight the night before the procedure. Get a good night's sleep, and be reassured about the procedure. Your routine medicines should be taken first thing in the morning, unless you are instructed otherwise. Because of the medicines used to make you sleepy, someone must come with you to the procedure and drive you home.

This handout provides a general overview on this subject and may not apply to everyone. Talk to your family doctor to find out if this information applies to you and to get more information.

PATIENT INSTRUCTIONS

Following Esophagogastroduodenoscopy (EGD)

1. You will be monitored in the office for a brief period after the procedure. Many people rest or sleep during this time. After you have been monitored, the heart and oxygen monitors will be discontinued. Your doctor will discuss the results of the exam with you and whoever comes with you.

2. You may be sleepy as you return home. You must have someone drive you home, and we request that someone stay with you for a few hours if you need to sleep off the medicines. Please have the person watching you call the office after a few hours and tell us how you are doing.

3. You must avoid alcoholic beverages for at least the rest of the day after the procedure. Do not take any tranquilizers, anxiety medicines, or sleeping pills for at least 1 day after the procedure, because they can react with the medicines used during the EGD procedure.

4. The numbing medicine in your throat will wear off in a few hours. It is safe to start drinking fluids after it has completely worn off. Many people experience a sore throat after the procedure because the scope passed through that area. The sore throat wears off gradually over the next few days and can be helped by drinking icy cold fluids.

5. If you feel sick to your stomach or vomit, don't try to eat anything. Usually it is the medicines, and not the actual procedure, that makes people feel sick. This usually passes as the medicine wears off.

6. Please do not drive or operate any machinery for 8 hours after the procedure. Most people feel like eating about 4 hours after the procedure.

7. EGD is a very safe procedure, but complications have been reported (rarely). If you have any dizziness, fever, chest pain, severe abdominal discomfort, black stools, vomit blood, or have persistent vomiting, please call your doctor.

8. The doctor's office should contact you with the results of the biopsies performed during the examination. Usually, you will be called with the results in the next week. If you have not heard from our office 2 weeks after the procedure, please call.

9. Sometimes a bacterial infection that causes ulcers is detected in the stomach. If you have the infection, you may be asked to take medicine. We will give you further instructions if the infection is detected.

INFORMED CONSENT FORM

Esophagogastroduodenoscopy (EGD)

PATIENT: ______________________________

DATE: __________________

1. I hereby authorize Dr. ______________ to perform the procedure known as esophagogastroduodenoscopy (EGD).

2. I understand that this is a procedure to examine my esophagus (swallowing tube), stomach, and the duodenum (first portion of my small intestine). I understand that a small, flexible lighted tube will be placed into my stomach. I understand that my physician will give me numbing medication for my throat, and that additional medication may be given in the form of a tablet, nasal spray, or intravenous fluid to help me to relax for the procedure. I understand that my heart, breathing, and oxygenation will be monitored during the procedure. My physician wants me to be relaxed but awake for the procedure, so that I can aid with the swallowing of the tube. I understand that the practice of medicine is not an exact science, and that no guarantee can be made regarding the outcome of my planned procedure.

3. My doctor has explained that this procedure is generally safe, but that certain risks accompany any procedure. Risks associated with this study include:
   - Bleeding, sometimes requiring transfusion or hospitalization
   - Pain associated with the procedure, or sore throat afterward
   - Allergic reaction to the medications used for the procedure
   - Aspiration of fluid into the lungs after vomiting
   - Perforation, or creating a hole, in any of the areas studied by this examination
   - Respiratory arrest, or stopping breathing, during or after the procedure
   - Rare, unusual reactions, including possible death from any surgical procedure

4. I understand that there are alternatives to this procedure, including x-ray examinations. I understand that I can refuse this procedure.

5. I understand that unforeseen conditions may alter the planned procedure. I give permission to my doctor to alter the procedure (such as to perform brushings of a lesion), if necessary, or to administer additional anesthetics or other medication if I should need them for the completion of my procedure.

6. I have read this form and other sheets given to me by my physician. I have had my questions answered to my satisfaction.

WITNESS: ____________________

PATIENT: ____________________

DATE: ____________________

MINOR: ____________________

PARENT: ____________________

NURSING INSTRUCTIONS

Esophagogastroduodenoscopy

PREPROCEDURE SETUP

The EGD nursing checklist should be used as a guide for the setup and completion of the procedure.

The scope should be prepared, and the channels tested before the patient is brought to the examination room. Confirm the availability and functioning of resuscitation equipment and oxygen.

Orient the patient to the room and equipment. Assist the patient with gown placement.

Absorbable pads should be placed over the pillow, and then over the patient's left shoulder once the patient lies down in the left lateral decubitus position.

Oximetry, cardiac and blood pressure monitoring is initiated.

NONSTERILE TRAY

Place the following items on a nonsterile sheet covering the Mayo stand:

Nonsterile gloves and mask
1 inch of 4 × 4 gauze
Butorphanol spray (Stadol)
Medicine cup filled with 10 mL viscous 2% lidocaine (Xylocaine) mixed with fruit (watermelon) flavoring
A disposable plastic spoon for administering the viscous lidocaine
Benzocaine 20% spray (Hurricaine)
2 CLOtest testing wells
1 inch of 2% lidocaine jelly on 4 × 4 gauze (for scope lubrication)
Mouth guard

ENDOSCOPY CART

The EGD scope is connected to the light source, camera, and video screen.
Suction and water channels are connected and tested for proper functioning.

Biopsy forceps
Oximetry monitor
Cardiac monitor with leads
Automated blood pressure recording unit

PROCEDURE AND POSTPROCEDURE INSTRUCTIONS

Record vital signs on the nursing checklist form.

Hold the patient's head steady, and assist with neck flexion to facilitate intubation.

Assist with the performance of the biopsies.

Notify the physician immediately of any EKG or oximetry monitoring changes.

Assist the physician in cleaning the secretions off the patient's cheek at the completion of the procedure.

Secure the safety of the patient by continuing monitoring, if needed, and raising side rails.

Initiate endoscope, biopsy forceps, and equipment cleaning.

Disconnect the monitoring equipment when monitoring is no longer needed.

Dispose of soiled gauze and absorbent pads in an appropriate biohazard container.

Complete paperwork, including pathology forms for biopsies.

NURSING CHECKLIST

Esophagogastroduodenoscopy

NAME: ______________________________

AGE: ______________

DATE: ______________

PREPROCEDURE

____ 1. Prepare the scope: test the water channel, suction channel, clarity of the picture.
____ 2. Orient the patient to the room and equipment. Assist the patient with gown placement. The patient can be seated on the table.
____ 3. Answer any patient questions, and have the patient sign the informed consent form.
____ 4. Confirm that the patient has been NPO.
____ 5. Confirm that the patient has someone present to take him or her home.
____ 6. Remove dentures or partial plates.
____ 7. Place EKG monitoring leads and initiate cardiac monitoring.
____ 8. Initiate oximetry monitoring.
____ 9. Confirm availability of properly functioning resuscitation equipment and oxygen.
____10. Prepare the equipment tray, biopsy forceps, and topical anesthetic solutions.
____11. Insert IV (if desired by the physician).

PROCEDURE

____ 1. Assist with intranasal butorphanol (Stadol) administration: ____ 1 or ____ 2 sprays
____ 2. Record vital signs (below).
____ 3. Assist with administration of topical anesthetics.
____ 4. Hold the patient's head steady, and assist with neck flexion to facilitate intubation.
____ 5. Record the time of scope insertion.
____ 6. Notify the physician immediately of EKG or oximetry changes.
____ 7. Assist with obtaining and processing biopsies.
____ 8. Assist with photography (if desired). Record the time of scope withdrawal.

POSTPROCEDURE

____ 1. Assist the physician in cleaning secretions off cheek, rolling the patient to the back.
____ 2. Secure the safety of the patient, raise side rails if available.
____ 3. Disconnect monitoring equipment. Complete vital signs and paperwork.
____ 4. Initiate scope cleaning.
____ 5. Disconnect IV fluids, if used.
____ 6. Assist the patient with dressing; prepare the patient for the physician conference.

	Time	Pulse	Respirations	Blood Pressure
Baseline				
Start				
Mid-Procedure				
Mid-Procedure				
Mid-Procedure				
End				

Record the temperature at the start of the procedure if the patient has had any recent infections or illness.

PREPROCEDURE COUNSELING FORM

Esophagogastroduodenoscopy

PATIENT NAME: ______________________________

DATE: ______________

AGE: ______________

Medication allergies: ______________________
Current medications: ______________________
Active medical problems: ______________________
Prior GI diagnoses: ______________________

Circle All That Apply:

Smoking?	Yes	No	Dentures?	Yes	No
Prior ulcer?	Yes	No	NSAID use?	Yes	No
Nausea?	Yes	No	Vomiting?	Yes	No
Chest pain?	Yes	No	Abdominal pain?	Yes	No
Hoarseness?	Yes	No	Dysphagia?	Yes	No
Odynophagia?	Yes	No	Foul taste?	Yes	No
Wheezing?	Yes	No	Hematemesis?	Yes	No
Heartburn?	Yes	No	Bloating?	Yes	No
Belching?	Yes	No	Melena?	Yes	No
Chronic cough?	Yes	No	Diabetes?	Yes	No
AIDS?	Yes	No	Artificial heart valve?	Yes	No
Iron deficiency?	Yes	No	Diarrhea?	Yes	No

Symptoms present for how long: ______________

UGI performed? Yes No When?

____

Prior EGD? Yes No When?

____

GI medications taken: ______________
Impression:

Plan: Patient is an appropriate candidate for EGD. Anesthesia options reviewed.
Risks, benefits of the procedure reviewed.
Patient agrees to sedation with oral benzodiazepines/intranasal butorphanol.

- ____ Complications reviewed: Bleeding, aspiration, sore throat, perforation, infection, medication reaction, respiratory arrest.
- ____ Anatomy and procedure description reviewed.
- ____ Anti-reflux recommendations: Avoid offending foods, avoid chocolates and mints, elevate head of bed, weight reduction, low-fat diet.
- ____ Smoking cessation urged.
- ____ NSAIDs discontinued.
- ____ Benzodiazepine sample/prescription given for oral preprocedure sedation.

Physician: ______________
CC: ______________

PROCEDURE RECORDING FORM

Esophagogastroduodenoscopy

PATIENT NAME: ______________________________

DATE: ____________________

Counseling performed: ____________________
Procedure indication: ____________________
Procedure anesthesia (check and circle medications given):

- ____ Triazolam 0.25 or 0.5 mg
- ____ Intranasal butorphanol sprays 1 or 2
- ____ Lidocaine 2% solution
- ____ Topical benzocaine 20% spray
- ____ IV administered with: ____________________
- ____ Monitoring of oximetry, cardiac tracing, blood pressure

Procedure Description: The patient gave informed consent for the procedure. Cardiac and oximetry monitors were attached to the skin, and the patient was placed in the left lateral decubitus position. Topical anesthesia was administered to the hypopharynx, and additional sedation administered only if needed for patient relaxation. The neck was flexed down to the chest, and the mouth guard was gently inserted between the upper and lower teeth. The scope was lubricated, and then passed inside the mouth guard and over the tongue. The hypopharynx and larynx were visualized, and the scope passed into the esophagus. Upon reaching the distal esophagus, the GE junction was visualized, and the diaphragmatic indentation noted by the sniff test. The scope was passed into the stomach, and the gastric lake suctioned. The scope was passed through the pylorus, and maneuvered into the descending duodenum. The duodenum and duodenal bulb were thoroughly examined with scope withdrawal back into the stomach. Biopsies were performed in the distal stomach for *Helicobacter pylori* testing. The gastric mucosa was thoroughly inspected, and the scope retroflexed to view the cardia. The sniff test was repeated. Air was suctioned from the stomach, and the scope withdrawn into the esophagus. The esophageal mucosa was thoroughly inspected. The scope was removed from the patient, and the patient tolerated the procedure well. Monitoring revealed adequate cardiac and oxygenation status. The patient was informed of the procedure results.

Areas not well visualized: ____________________
Biopsies: ____________________
Complications: ____________________
Circle abnormalities noted:
Description and location:

Ulcer	Glycogenic acanthosis
Erosion	Diverticulum
Tumor	Hiatal hernia
Stricture	Angiodysplasia
Erythema	Gastric bile
Varices	Bleeding
Scarring	Friability
Polyp	Submucosal lesion
Other	

Diagnoses:

Plan:

Physician: ____________________
CC: ____________________

CHAPTER 4

Flexible Sigmoidoscopy

PATIENT INFORMATION

Flexible Sigmoidoscopy

What is flexible sigmoidoscopy?

Flexible sigmoidoscopy is a way to look at the colon (large bowel) using a flexible, lighted tube to see the inside of the bowel for any abnormal growths or inflammation of the colon wall. The anal canal also is examined with a short tube as part of this examination for colon diseases.

What are the benefits of flexible sigmoidoscopy?

Flexible sigmoidoscopy is an effective tool to prevent and detect early colon cancer. Colon cancer is the second most common cause of cancer death in the United States. Many lives can be saved if precancerous growths (polyps) are discovered before they become cancerous, or if colon cancer is discovered before it has spread. Sigmoidoscopy also can diagnose inflammation of the colon from diseases such as ulcerative colitis or Crohn's disease. Other colon conditions such as diverticulosis also can be diagnosed.

Who should have the procedure?

People who have problems such as persistent abdominal pain, rectal bleeding, persistent diarrhea, or anemia (low blood counts) may need flexible sigmoidoscopy. All individuals (even without complaints) over the age of 50 should undergo the exam every 3 to 5 years to screen for colon diseases.

How should I prepare for the procedure?

Consume a clear liquid diet the afternoon and evening the day before the scheduled sigmoidoscopy. Take two Fleet enemas at home just before the examination. Your doctor will tell you how to prepare.

Is the exam uncomfortable?

The exam produces some discomfort and abdominal pressure. Air is placed in the colon to allow for viewing, and the air can produce cramping. Most people tolerate the exam well and prefer not to be sedated so that they can resume normal activities immediately afterwards. People who are sedated have a slightly increased risk of colon perforation (a hole created in the wall of the colon). The short exam time (usually 5 to 20 minutes) helps make this a tolerable procedure.

Are biopsies performed during sigmoidoscopy?

Most procedures do not require biopsies, but occasionally a biopsy of a growth is needed. The biopsy is performed by clipping a small piece of tissue inside the colon and removing it through the viewing tube. If a biopsy is performed, you may have some minimal discomfort or slight bleeding from the rectum for several days.

This handout provides a general overview on this subject and may not apply to everyone. Talk to your family doctor to find out if this information applies to you and to get more information.

PATIENT INFORMATION

Preparing for Flexible Sigmoidoscopy

1. You may have a clear liquid diet the afternoon and the evening before the examination. This includes broth, juices, clear beverages, and clear soups.

2. Please avoid taking aspirin, iron pills, or the blood-thinning medicine called Coumadin for one week prior to the procedure.

3. Please purchase two Fleet enemas at any pharmacy. These should be used the day of the exam. The first enema is given 2 hours before the scheduled exam. The second enema is given 1 hour before the scheduled exam. Try to hold each enema for several minutes, and then evacuate the bowel completely.

4. Arrive at the office at least 20 minutes before the scheduled exam. Let the nurse know if you do not think your bowel was completely emptied, or if the second enema still produced a large amount of solid stool.

5. If you are diabetic and take insulin, please take your usual insulin dose the morning of the procedure. Make up your calories with clear liquids as you would on a sick-day diet. You can check your blood sugar frequently, and carry juice with you if you should develop hypoglycemia.

This handout provides a general overview on this subject and may not apply to everyone. Talk to your family doctor to find out if this information applies to you and to get more information.

PATIENT INSTRUCTIONS

Following Flexible Sigmoidoscopy

1. You may feel full of air and feel discomfort following the procedure. You will be offered the opportunity to go to the bathroom immediately after the procedure or once you have dressed.

2. Your doctor will return and discuss the findings of the examination. Feel free to ask any questions you may have.

3. You should be able to drive yourself home following the procedure, unless you required additional sedative medications (oral sedatives or intravenous medicines) for completion of the procedure.

4. You will probably continue to note air and cramping once you leave the office. Walking can help to eliminate excess air left in your colon following the procedure.

5. You can help relieve any discomfort after the procedure by taking ibuprofen (brand names: Advil, Motrin, Nuprin), three 200-mg tablets three times a day with food, or acetaminophen (brand name: Tylenol), two 325-mg tablets every 4 hours.

6. The rare, but more severe, complications of sigmoidoscopy usually produce severe abdominal pain, vomiting, and an enlarging abdomen. If any of these symptoms occur, or if you don't feel well following the procedure, please call your doctor's office right away.

7. Minimal bleeding into the stools can be noted after flexible sigmoidoscopy. If the scope slides past a hemorrhoid or if biopsies are performed, then bleeding is more likely. If you have excessive bleeding or pass large blood clots in the stool, contact your doctor's office right away.

INFORMED CONSENT FORM

Flexible Sigmoidoscopy

PATIENT: ______________________________

DATE: ____________________

1. I hereby authorize Dr. ____________________ to perform the procedure known as flexible sigmoidoscopy.

2. I understand that this is a procedure performed to examine the inside of my colon or large intestine. The three parts of the procedure are designed to examine the left colon, the rectum, and the anal canal. The first part of the examination is performed with a gloved finger, lubricating the anal canal and feeling for tumors. The second part of the examination is with a short clear tube that allows viewing of the anal canal. The major, third portion of the examination uses a long, flexible, fiberoptic lighted tube that allows for viewing inside the colon.

   I understand that most people tolerate the examination without requiring anesthesia, but sometimes the examination must be discontinued due to patient discomfort. I understand that the practice of medicine is not an exact science, and that no guarantee can be made regarding the outcome of my planned procedure.

3. My doctor has explained to me that this procedure is generally safe, but that certain risks accompany any surgical procedure. Some of the risks associated with flexible sigmoidoscopy include:
   - Bleeding from the scope sliding past a vascular area, such as a hemorrhoid
   - Perforation (the scope creates a hole in the wall of the colon)
   - Dizziness or lightheadedness during or after the procedure
   - Discomfort or pain
   - Infection introduced into the colon by the lighted tube (rare)
   - Allergic reaction to the numbing medicine or instruments used in the procedure
   - Rare, unusual reactions, including possible death following any surgical procedure

4. I understand that there are alternatives to this procedure, including barium enema, colonoscopy, stool testing for blood, CT scanning, or no colon exam at all. I understand that I can refuse this procedure.

5. I understand that unforeseen conditions may alter the planned procedure. I give permission to my doctor to alter the procedure (such as to examine transverse colon if the scope easily passes that far), if necessary, or to administer additional anesthetics or other medication if I should need them for completion of the examination.

6. I have read this form and other sheets given to me by my physician. I have had my questions answered to my satisfaction.

WITNESS: ____________________

PATIENT: ____________________

DATE: ____________________

MINOR: ____________________

PARENT: ____________________

NURSING INSTRUCTIONS

Flexible Sigmoidoscopy

PATIENT PREPARATION

Confirm that the patient performed the recommended enemas and preparation

The patient removes clothing from below the waistline, and is seated on the examination table with a disposable sheet draped over the legs. Place an absorbent sheet beneath the patient on the table.

NONSTERILE TRAY FOR THE PROCEDURE

Place the following items on a nonsterile drape covering on a Mayo stand:

2 or 3 nonsterile gloves (some physicians double-glove the right hand and remove the outer glove after the rectal examination and anoscopy)

1 inch of 4 × 4 gauze

1 inch of water-soluble (K-Y) jelly dispensed on one corner of the drape

1 inch of 5% lidocaine ointment (Xylocaine) dispensed on one corner of the drape

An emesis basin filled with water for suction at the end of the procedure

Ives anoscope

ENDOSCOPY CART

Water bottle is filled and connected to the light source.

The suction unit is plugged into the wall outlet and connected to the scope.

The light source is plugged into the wall outlet, and the sigmoidoscope is connected to the light source.

The operation of the sigmoidoscope should be checked before the procedure: air should be bubbled into the basin of water, and some of the water suctioned through.

Biopsy forceps should be available (if in sterile packaging, do not open unless the forceps are needed).

POSTPROCEDURE NURSING INSTRUCTIONS

Offer the patient the opportunity to go to the bathroom immediately after the procedure.

Once the patient dresses, move the patient to a chair or another room for counseling with the physician.

Refer to the cleaning/disinfection sheet for instructions in performing endoscope cleaning and maintenance.

Soiled gauze is appropriately disposed of in a biohazard waste container.

Soiled sheets should be placed in an appropriate container.

Clean the anoscope and biopsy forceps (if used) and place in packaging for sterilization in the steam sterilizer.

NURSING INSTRUCTIONS

Cleaning and Disinfecting the GI Endoscope

1. Water is suctioned through the endoscope immediately after the procedure is completed to prevent stool from clogging the suction channel.

2. The suction channel is brushed, and then water is suctioned through again.

3. The scope is placed in a mild detergent solution, keeping the control head out of the water. The external sheath of the scope is washed with a sponge.

4. The biopsy, suction, and air/water valves are removed and cleaned.

5. The control head is wiped clean with a damp cloth, but not immersed.

6. The biopsy channel is brushed and cleaned with a detergent solution.

7. The entire scope is rinsed with tap water, and all channels are flushed with water.

8. Approximately 50 mL of disinfectant (glutaraldehyde [Cidex]) is suctioned through the biopsy channel.

9. The water insufflation bottle is partially filled with the disinfectant solution, and glutaraldehyde is flushed through the air/water channel.

10. The scope is placed in the disinfectant tray for at least 10 to 20 minutes. Avoid immersion of the control head.

11. The biopsy forceps are mechanically cleaned and soaked for at least 10 to 20 minutes in glutaraldehyde.

12. The scope is rinsed with water, and the biopsy channel flushed with water for 60 seconds.

13. The water bottle is rinsed with tap water, and the air/water channel is flushed with water for 60 seconds.

14. The exterior of the scope is rinsed again with tap water.

15. The umbilical cord is wiped with glutaraldehyde, and then wiped off with a wet towel.

16. Air is suctioned through the biopsy and air/water channels for 60 seconds.

17. The valves are dried with cotton-tipped swabs or left to air dry.

18. The scope is hung vertically to air dry. The water bottle is left open to air dry.

PROCEDURE RECORDING FORM

Flexible Sigmoidoscopy

PATIENT NAME: ____________________

DATE: ____________________

AGE: ____________________

Personal History of:

Rectal bleeding?	Yes	No	Hemorrhoids?	Yes	No
Rectal pain?	Yes	No	Constipation?	Yes	No
Black stools?	Yes	No	Colon polyps?	Yes	No
Diverticular disease?	Yes	No	Colon surgery?	Yes	No
Diarrhea?	Yes	No	Anemia?	Yes	No
Prior hysterectomy?	Yes	No	Abdominal pain?	Yes	No
Change in stools?	Yes	No	Colon cancer?	Yes	No
Inflammatory bowel dis.?	Yes	No	Weight loss?	Yes	No

Family History in a 1st-Degree Relative With:

Colon cancer?	Yes	No	Colon polyps?	Yes	No

List the Date and Findings:
Prior flex. sig.: ____________________
Ba. enema: ____________________
Colonoscopy: ____________________
Antibiotic prophylaxis for artificial valves or joints: Yes ____ No ____

Indications for Procedure: Colon CA Screening and Evaluation of:

Prostate examination if male: ____________________
Colon prep.: ____________________
Hemorrhoids: ____________________
Polyps: ____________________

Inserted to ____ cm
Pt. tolerance: ____________________
Diverticula: ____________________
Complications: ____________________

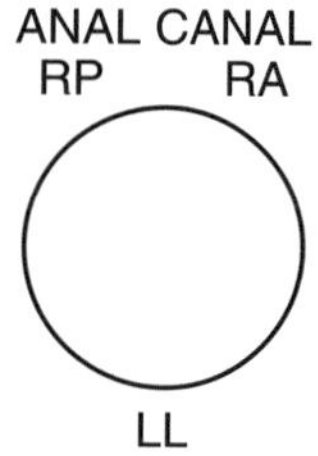

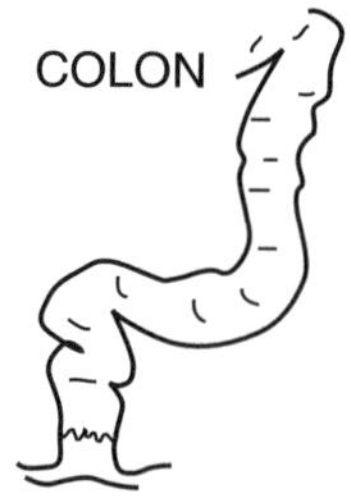

Impression:

Plan:

Repeat sigmoidoscopy in 3 to 5 years.

Offered barium enema to visualize R colon.

High fiber diet.

Postprocedure instruction sheet given.

Physician: ____________________
CC: ____________________

CHAPTER 5

Lumbar Puncture

PATIENT INFORMATION

Lumbar Puncture

What is lumbar puncture?

Lumbar puncture is a commonly performed medical procedure done to check the spinal fluid that circulates in the spinal canal and around the brain. A needle is inserted into the back, and fluid is withdrawn for analysis. The lower back is the safest location for needle entry. To allow the needle to slip between the bones of the lower back (vertebrae), you will be asked to lie on your side and curl into a ball. An assistant will help you to stay in this position for the several minutes required to complete the procedure.

Why is lumbar puncture performed?

Lumbar puncture is done to make a diagnosis. The most common reason for the test is to rule out the possibility of infection around the brain (meningitis). Lumbar puncture is also performed to check for bleeding around the brain, cancer, or multiple sclerosis. Lumbar puncture is occasionally performed for treatment such as to administer cancer treatment medicine into the fluid around the brain.

Is the procedure uncomfortable?

The procedure can be somewhat uncomfortable, as can any procedure that requires a needle-stick. However, the skin will be numbed with a small needle before the placement of the larger spinal needle. Sometimes the needle slips in immediately with no discomfort. In other situations, the needle has to be guided in past bony or arthritic areas and can make the procedure more uncomfortable.

Are there risks to this procedure?

Lumbar puncture is generally safe, but there are risks. The lower back is the safest location for needle insertion, but the needle can injure nerves and produce pain and abnormal sensation down into the legs. The procedure can produce pain in the back, bleeding, or (rarely) introduce infection into the spinal fluid. However, it is much more important to diagnose your medical condition than to be overly concerned with the risks that can accompany this procedure.

Will I get a headache following the procedure?

Up to 25% of people develop a headache following lumbar puncture. The headache may be worse when you are standing or sitting. The headache is believed to be related to leaking of some of the spinal fluid into the tissues of the back at the needle insertion site. Lying flat on your back or stomach for 4 hours following the procedure may help prevent the headache.

This handout provides a general overview on this subject and may not apply to everyone. Talk to your family doctor to find out if this information applies to you and to get more information.

PATIENT INSTRUCTIONS

Following Lumbar Puncture

1. Your doctor may rub your back at the puncture site immediately following the procedure. A bandage will be placed over the needle insertion site. You may remove it after 4 hours.

2. The most common complication associated with lumbar puncture is postprocedure headache. This occurs in 5 to 25% of patients. The headache may develop from a fluid leak into the tissues of the lower back at the needle insertion site. Fluid leakage may be greater if you resume regular activity right after the procedure. Lie flat (either on your stomach or back) for at least 4 hours following the procedure.

3. You can take ibuprofen (brand names: Advil, Motrin, Nuprin), three or four 200-mg tablets three times a day with food, or acetaminophen (brand name: Tylenol), two 325-mg tablets every 4 hours, if you experience discomfort in your back or a headache following the procedure.

4. Call your doctor if you continue to have a headache 24 hours after the procedure. Occasionally, people require treatment with a blood patch, using a small amount of your own blood, to stop the leakage of fluid in your lower back.

5. Call your doctor if you develop a problem after the procedure, such as a new fever, severe back pain, numbness or tingling in the legs, or weakness in the legs.

6. Your doctor will contact you with the test results on the fluid that was removed. Please continue taking any medicines as prescribed by your doctor.

INFORMED CONSENT FORM

Lumbar Puncture

PATIENT: ______________________________

DATE: ____________________

1. I hereby authorize Dr. ________________ to perform the procedure known as lumbar puncture.

2. I understand that this is a procedure performed under local anesthesia to analyze or remove fluid from the spinal canal in my lower back. I understand that the needle is inserted into the lower back because this is the area with the lowest risk of injuring nerves or other structures. I understand that insertion can be difficult, especially if I have arthritis in my lower back. I realize that the information obtained from this procedure can be important to my health care. I understand that the practice of medicine is not an exact science, and that no guarantee can be made regarding the outcome of my planned procedure.

3. My doctor has explained to me that this procedure is generally safe, but that certain risks accompany any surgical procedure. Risks associated with lumbar puncture include:

Bleeding at the needle insertion site

Nerve damage from the needle hitting a nerve, usually producing pain or altered sensations in the legs

Local pain in the back at the needle insertion site

Headache from the procedure, that can rarely persist for weeks

Infection introduced into the spinal canal, or meningitis from the procedure

Allergic reaction to the numbing medicine or surgical instruments

Rare, unusual reactions, including possible death following any surgical procedure

4. I understand that there are alternatives to this procedure, such as radiologic diagnostic tests like CT or MRI scans. Alternate tests may not provide the same information as lumbar puncture. I understand that I can refuse this procedure.

5. I understand that unforeseen conditions may alter the planned procedure. I give permission to my doctor to alter the procedure (such as to inject my blood into the skin of the back to cover a fluid leak after the lumbar puncture needle is withdrawn), if necessary, or to administer additional medications if I should need them for the completion of my procedure.

6. I have read this form and other sheets given to me by my physician. I have had my questions answered to my satisfaction.

WITNESS: ____________________

PATIENT: ____________________

DATE: ____________________

MINOR: ____________________

PARENT: ____________________

NURSING INSTRUCTIONS

Lumbar Puncture

PREPROCEDURE NURSING INSTRUCTIONS

The patient should have the shirt elevated to the level of the shoulder blades, and pants and underpants lowered or removed.

The patient is placed in the left lateral decubitus position. The patient's hips, knees, and neck are flexed toward the abdomen. The back should be vertical, and placed at the edge of the table.

The assistant should help maintain the patient in this position throughout the procedure. A long sheet can be placed behind the knees and neck, or the assistant can place an arm over each of these sites to assist the patient in holding still.

STERILE TRAY FOR THE PROCEDURE

Most physicians use a purchased sterile lumbar puncture tray.

The tray should be opened, folding back the edges of the paper wrapping and avoiding contamination of the items on the tray.

Once the tray is opened, povidone-iodine solution is poured into one of the empty plastic wells on the tray. The container of povidone-iodine solution must not contaminate the sterile tray.

Sterile gloves must be provided for the procedure.

POSTPROCEDURE NURSING INSTRUCTIONS

The back is cleansed of povidone-iodine solution and a sterile bandage is applied to the puncture site.

The patient's clothes are returned to their normal position, and the patient is laid flat, either on the back or stomach.

The needles are disposed of in an appropriate sharps container.

Soiled (bloody) gauze is disposed of in an appropriate biohazard waste container.

The remaining items on the tray, and the tray itself, are removed.

The nurse should check that the specimen containers are tightly sealed and labeled with appropriate patient information identifying the specimens, and that paperwork for the pathology evaluation has been completed.

PROCEDURE RECORDING FORM

Lumbar Puncture

PATIENT NAME: ______________________________

DATE: ______________

AGE: ______________

Preprocedure head CT result: ______________

Indications for the procedure: ______________

Circle the Correct Responses or Findings:

Headache?	Yes	No	Nuchal rigidity?	Yes	No
Fever?	Yes	No	Night sweats?	Yes	No
History of syphilis?	Yes	No	History of cancer?	Yes	No
Symptoms suggestive of MS?	Yes	No	Papilledema?	Yes	No
Coagulopathy?	Yes	No	Focal neurologic findings?	Yes	No
Findings sugg. of Guillain-Barré	Yes	No			

Procedure Description: The patient gave informed consent for the procedure. The patient was placed in the left lateral decubitus position. The hips, knees, and neck were flexed, and the back was placed in a vertical position near the edge of the table. The position was maintained with the help of an assistant. The superior aspect of the iliac crests were palpated, and the line between the crests was used to identify the L3-L4 interspace. The lumbar puncture tray was opened and sterile gloves applied. Povidone-iodine solution was used to cleanse the insertion site and surrounding skin. Sterile drapes were used to cover the entire lower back. The insertion site was reconfirmed by palpating the iliac crests and lumbar spinous processes through the sterile drape. Lidocaine 1% was administered intracuticular and then deep down into the interspinous ligament near the dura. The 21-gauge spinal needle was inserted in the midline between the spinous processes, angling the needle 20 degrees cephalad. The needle was inserted into the subarachnoid space, the stylet was withdrawn, and the opening pressure was obtained. The CSF fluid was obtained, the stylet was reinserted, and the needle was withdrawn. The site was rubbed for 15 seconds, and a bandage was applied. The patient tolerated the procedure well.

Opening pressure: ____ mm Hg (nl.<20 mm, equivocal 20–25, high >25)

Tube 1: Glucose, protein and ______________
Tube 2: Gram stain, bacterial culture and sensitivity and ______________
Tube 3: Cell count and differential and ______________
Tube 4: Hold fluid and ______________

Optional: Fungal culture, KOH examination, cytologic examination, AFB smears, Tb cultures, protein electrophoresis, VDRL, viral cultures, oligoclonal banding.

Complications: ______________________________
Impressions:

Plan:

Physician: ______________
CC: ______________

CHAPTER 6

Flexible Nasolaryngoscopy

PATIENT INFORMATION

Flexible Nasolaryngoscopy

What is flexible nasolaryngoscopy?

Flexible nasolaryngoscopy is an examination of your nose, voicebox, and upper respiratory tract. During the procedure, a small, flexible, fiberoptic scope (about half the width of a pencil) is inserted into one side of the nose, permitting your doctor to see the curves and small spaces of your nose and larynx.

Is the procedure painful?

Most people find the procedure to be relatively comfortable. Your doctor will use numbing medicine to make you as comfortable as possible. You may feel a tickling sensation when the scope is first placed inside your nose. The scope may be a little uncomfortable during brief periods of the exam, but most people find it very tolerable. Holding your head steady is important and allows your doctor to perform a thorough examination. Complications of the procedure are rare and mild, and include vomiting, bleeding, sneezing, coughing, or gagging.

How do I get ready for the procedure?

Do not eat for 4 hours before the procedure. However, you can take your regular medicines with water the day of the procedure. The exam can be performed on someone who has just eaten, but because of the gagging that occasionally accompanies the procedure, it is best to have an empty stomach.

What will happen during the procedure?

You will be seated upright for the exam. Your physician will spray your nose with a decongestant to shrink the nasal passages, and then spray an anesthetic to numb the tissues. Both medicines have a slightly bitter flavor, which you may taste for about 1 minute as they drain back into your throat. The medicines are not always required to perform the procedure, but may make the exam safer and more comfortable.

The scope will be slid to the back of the nose, and then down the throat to your voice box. You should breathe slowly through your open mouth. You will be asked to make certain sounds such as "K" or "E," especially when your vocal cords are being examined. If mucus blocks the tip of the scope, your doctor will ask you to swallow to remove the mucus and clear the view. As the scope is being withdrawn, your physician will examine your nose. This part of the exam can be uncomfortable but it is over quickly.

How long does the procedure last?

Flexible nasolaryngoscopy usually takes just a few minutes. If this exam reveals any significant problems, you may be asked to take medicine or see a nose or throat specialist. Most people do not require pain medicine after the procedure, and you should be able to resume normal activities right away. However, you should avoid eating or drinking until the numb feeling in your throat has worn off, and normal feeling has returned (about 2 hours).

This handout provides a general overview on this subject and may not apply to everyone. Talk to your family doctor to find out if this information applies to you and to get more information.

PATIENT INSTRUCTIONS

Following Flexible Nasolaryngoscopy

1. After the procedure, you may wish to blow your nose. You will be given tissue, but blow gently to avoid causing a nose bleed.

2. You should not eat or drink after the procedure until your throat stops feeling numb. It may take about 2 hours from the time you leave the office for you to have normal feeling in your nose and on your tongue.

3. No limitation of activity is necessary after the procedure. You should be able to drive yourself home after the procedure.

4. Most people do not need any pain medicine after the procedure.

5. Your doctor will discuss the findings of your examination immediately after the procedure. You may be asked to take medicine or to see another doctor for further care, depending on the findings.

6. Medicine Instructions:
   ____
   ____
   ____

INFORMED CONSENT FORM

Flexible Nasolaryngoscopy

PATIENT: ______________________________________

DATE: ________________________

1. I hereby authorize Dr. ____________________ to perform the procedure known as flexible nasolaryngoscopy.

2. I understand that this is a diagnostic examination of the inside of the nasal cavity, upper throat, and voice box area or larynx. I understand that the examination can diagnose many medical problems affecting the upper respiratory tract. The small lighted tube used for the examination is about half the thickness of a pencil and slips easily into the nose. The procedure is performed after the application of a decongestant spray and a numbing (anesthetic) spray. I understand that the practice of medicine is not an exact science, and that no guarantee can be made regarding the outcome of my planned procedure.

3. My doctor has explained to me that this procedure is generally safe, but that certain risks accompany any medical procedure. Risks associated with flexible nasolaryngoscopy include:

    Bleeding if the scope slides past a vascular area

    Pain associated with the procedure

    Allergic reaction to the medications used in the procedure

    Coughing, gagging, or choking from the procedure

    Introduction of infection from the procedure

    Rare, unusual reactions, including possible death following any surgical procedure

4. I understand that there are alternatives to this procedure, including radiology studies such as x-rays or CT scans. I understand that failure to undergo a diagnostic evaluation may result in the failure to diagnose a condition that I may have. I understand that I can refuse this procedure.

5. I understand that unforeseen conditions may alter the planned procedure. I give permission to my doctor to alter the procedure (such as to compress a bleeding site discovered in the procedure), if necessary, or to administer additional anesthetics or medications if I should need them for the completion of my procedure.

6. I have read this form and other sheets given to me by my physician. I have had my questions answered to my satisfaction.

WITNESS: ____________________________

PATIENT: ____________________________

DATE: ____________________________

MINOR: ____________________________

PARENT: ____________________________

NURSING INSTRUCTIONS

Flexible Nasolaryngoscopy

PATIENT PREPARATION

The patient is seated on an electric table, if available, and the upper portion of the table is raised to support the patient's back and head (manually raise the head on nonelectric tables). The base of the table is then raised so that the patient's head is just below or at the same height as the examiner's head. The patient is given tissues to hold in one hand and an emesis basin to hold in the other hand. An absorbent sheet can be draped over the patient's shoulders and tucked inside the patient's collar.

NONSTERILE TRAY FOR THE PROCEDURE

A drape is placed on a Mayo stand and the following items placed on top:

1 inch of 4% lidocaine jelly (Xylocaine) on a corner of the drape (for scope lubrication)

Bottle of oxymetazoline hydrochloride 0.05% (Afrin) spray

4% lidocaine solution in an atomizer spray bottle

1 inch of nonsterile 4 × 4-inch gauze

ENDOSCOPY CART

Flexible fiberoptic nasolaryngoscope (3.5 mm outer diameter) attached to the light source

Suction machine should be available if needed

POSTPROCEDURE NURSING INSTRUCTIONS

The patient is offered the opportunity to blow his or her nose, and is advised to do so gently.

The drape, tissue, and emesis basin are removed from the patient.

The patient can be moved from the examination table to a chair for the postprocedure counseling with the physician.

The oxymetazoline spray nozzle is wiped clean and the bottle is stored for the next use (as long as no patient contact was made with the nozzle tip during administration).

The spray nozzle of the atomizer bottle is washed, rinsed, and soaked in glutaraldehyde (Cidex) for at least 10 to 20 minutes. The nozzle is rinsed thoroughly, dried, and lidocaine is sprayed through the nozzle before the bottle is stored.

The endoscope is cleaned and disinfected in the following manner:

Wash the immersion tube portion of the scope with soap and warm water.

Immerse the insertion tube in glutaraldehyde for a minimum of 10 to 20 minutes.

Wipe off the umbilical cord and instrument head with glutaraldehyde and then water.

Rinse the scope thoroughly with water and then dry the scope.

Hang the scope upright in a safe location after each use.

PROCEDURE RECORDING FORM

Flexible Nasolaryngoscopy

PATIENT NAME: ____

AGE: ____________________

DATE: ____________________

Indications for the Study (Circle All That Apply):

nasal congestion hoarseness acid laryngitis chronic rhinorrhea
cancer screening chronic cough chronic pharyngeal pain bleeding / epistaxis
halitosis eustachian tube dysfunction postnasal drainage nasal polyps
chronic facial pain dysphagia smoker globus sensation other ____________________

Patient gave informed consent for the procedure: Yes No
Preprocedure medications (circle which apply): oxymetazoline 0.05% / 4% lidocaine

Patient tolerance: ____________________
Complications: ____________________
Mucosal appearance: ____________________
Postprocedure instruction sheet given? Yes No

Indicate Structures Visualized: Check = normal; blank = not visualized; describe abnormalities

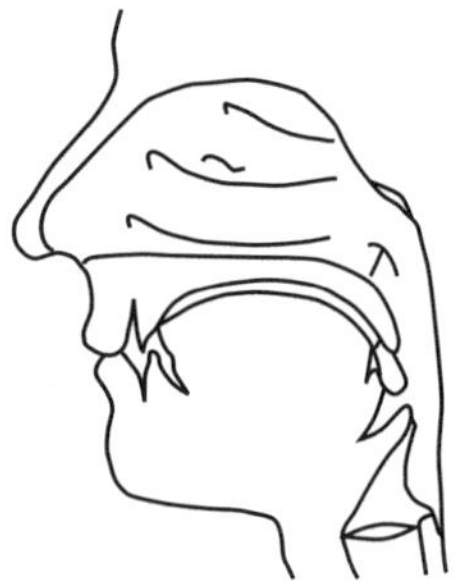

Left

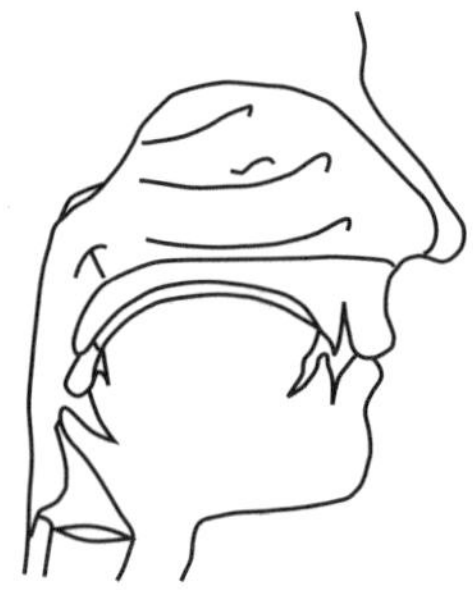

Right

_____ Septum _____
_____ Inferior turbinate _____
_____ Middle turbinate _____
_____ Superior turbinate _____
_____ Maxillary sinus orifice _____
_____ Sphenoid sinus orifice _____
_____ Eustachian tube orifice _____
_____ Adenoids _____
_____ Lingual tonsil _____
_____ Palatine tonsil _____
_____ Piriform sinuses _____
_____ Valleculae _____
_____ Vocal cords _____

Diagnosis:

Plan:

Physician: ____________________
CC: ____________________

CHAPTER 7

Simple Open Breast Biopsy

PATIENT INFORMATION

Simple Open Breast Biopsy

What is a simple open breast biopsy?

The simple open breast biopsy procedure removes a portion of tissue or a lump from the breast for analysis. The procedure is most commonly performed to find out if there is cancer in a lump in the breast. Anesthetic (numbing medicine) is administered into the breast, the growth is cut free, and the wound is closed with sutures (stitches).

What happens once the tissue is removed from the breast?

The tissue is sent to the hospital laboratory where it is examined under the microscope by a specialist physician known as a pathologist. Special studies may be performed on the tissue, such as checking for hormone receptors in the cells. Your doctor will notify you of the results of the laboratory studies as soon as they are available.

Is this procedure uncomfortable?

The administration of the local anesthetic or numbing medicine before the procedure can cause some discomfort. However, your doctor will try to completely numb the breast on all sides of the lesion. If you feel any discomfort during the procedure, additional anesthetic will be given. Overall, this simple procedure produces very little discomfort.

If you need it, medicine may be prescribed to reduce any discomfort you may experience.

Can this procedure be performed in the doctor's office?

Open breast biopsy can be safely and effectively performed in the doctor's office. Biopsy in the office setting can be performed at significant cost savings over procedures in the hospital. Office biopsies are generally performed for low-risk or noncancerous lesions. Approximately 82% of all breast biopsies performed in the United States reveal benign (not cancer) growths.

Do all breast biopsies have to be performed by a breast surgery specialist?

Simple open breast biopsy is straightforward and simple. If the initial testing (mammogram and needle biopsy) suggests the presence of cancer, the patient is generally referred to a breast surgeon right away. If the mammogram and needle biopsy suggest that the lump is benign (not cancer) disease, the lump can be safely removed by the simple biopsy technique performed in the office of your family physician.

This handout provides a general overview on this subject and may not apply to everyone. Talk to your family doctor to find out if this information applies to you and to get more information.

PATIENT INSTRUCTIONS

Following Simple Open Breast Biopsy

1. Your doctor will ask you to hold pressure to the surgery site for about 10 minutes following the procedure. You will be given some gauze to apply the pressure. Antibiotic cream is then applied to the wound, and gauze is taped over the site. The bulky dressing can be supported with a firm bra. Please wear a firm, supportive bra for the next 24 hours, and then during the day for the next week.

2. Bruising commonly follows the breast biopsy procedure. Sometimes the entire breast may appear black and blue. If a large, painful, blood clot develops beneath the wound, it may need to be drained with a needle. If you notice that the breast is increasing in size, the swelling is extensive, or your wound bleeds briskly, please call your doctor.

3. You may have some discomfort after the procedure. You can take a combination of acetaminophen (brand name: Tylenol), two 325 mg tablets every four hours, and ibuprofen (brand names: Advil, Motrin, Nuprin), three 200 mg tablets three times a day with food. Additional pain medications are rarely needed.

4. Infection can sometimes develop at any surgical site. If you notice increasing redness, warmth, pus drainage, or tenderness from the breast, please call your doctor.

5. The gauze can be removed the morning after the surgery, or sooner if it becomes soaked with blood. Band-Aids or gauze can be applied to the site every day. The deep sutures (stitches) are absorbed and do not need to be removed, but your doctor will want to remove the tape and recheck the breast in 7 to 10 days.

6. Your doctor's office will contact you with the results of the pathology evaluation performed on the tissue removed from your breast. These results will be reviewed with you if you are asked to return for removal of any skin sutures that may have been used.

7. Despite reassuring results from the biopsy, you can still develop breast cancer at a later time. You should continue to have cancer screening (breast examinations and mammography) as directed by your doctor.

INFORMED CONSENT FORM

Simple Open Breast Biopsy

PATIENT: ____________________

DATE: ____________________

1. I hereby authorize Dr. ____________________ to perform the procedure known as simple open breast biopsy.

2. I understand that this is a surgical procedure performed under local anesthesia to remove tissue from my breast. I understand that this procedure is usually performed to evaluate the tissue for the presence of cancer. This procedure also can be performed for therapeutic reasons, such as to remove an area causing persistent tenderness. The biopsy will attempt to remove the abnormal breast tissue with the least possible scarring, but I understand that the appearance of the breast may be altered by any surgical procedure. I understand that the practice of medicine is not an exact science, and that no guarantee can be made regarding the outcome of my planned procedure.

3. My doctor has explained to me that this procedure is generally safe, but that certain risks accompany any surgical procedure. Risks associated with the simple open breast biopsy procedure include:

Bleeding and bruising of the breast tissue, sometimes requiring drainage

Pain associated with the surgery or the healing process

Excessive scarring or depressions in the breast following the surgery

Allergic reaction to the numbing medication or the surgical instruments

Infection in the breast following the procedure

Failure to remove all of the abnormal growth, or removal of an alternate growth

Rare, unusual reactions, including possible death following any surgical procedure

4. I understand that there are alternatives to this procedure, including more extensive procedures performed by breast surgeons, or biopsy performed by radiologists with x-ray guidance. I understand that I can refuse this procedure.

5. I understand that unforeseen conditions may alter the planned procedure. I give permission to my doctor to alter the procedure (such as to place deep sutures to control bleeding), if necessary, or to administer additional anesthetics or other medications if I should need them for the completion of my procedure.

6. I have read this form and other sheets given to me by my physician. I have had my questions answered to my satisfaction.

WITNESS: ____________________

PATIENT: ____________________

DATE: ____________________

MINOR: ____________________

PARENT: ____________________

NURSING INSTRUCTIONS

Simple Open Breast Biopsy

PREPROCEDURE NURSING INSTRUCTIONS

An absorbent sheet is placed on the table beneath the surgical site.

The patient is asked to undress from the waist up and is given a gown. The patient lies supine on the surgical table. A sheet can be laid over the patient's abdomen to assist with patient comfort and privacy through the procedure.

NONSTERILE TRAY FOR ANESTHESIA

Place the following items on a nonsterile sheet covering a Mayo stand:

- Nonsterile gloves
- Skin marking pen
- 1 inch of 4 × 4 gauze
- Povidone-iodine solution placed on gauze
- 10-mL syringe filled with 2% lidocaine with epinephrine (Xylocaine with Epinephrine)
- Short (3/4-inch) 30-gauge needle and a long (1 1/4-inch) 27-gauge needle

STERILE TRAY FOR THE PROCEDURE

Place the following items on a sterile drape covering a Mayo stand:

- Sterile gloves
- 2 inches of sterile 4 × 4 gauze
- No. 15 scalpel and blade handle
- 3 hemostats
- Iris scissors
- Allis tissue forceps
- Metzenbaum (or other tissue-cutting) scissors
- Needle holder
- Adson forceps with teeth
- Adson forceps without teeth
- 4-0 Vicryl suture (or other absorbable suture)
- 5-0 Prolene suture (or other nonabsorbable suture)
- Disposable (nonsterile) battery cautery, inserted into a sterile glove
- Sterile 10-mL syringe, 18-gauge needle, and 27-gauge needle for additional anesthesia if needed

POSTPROCEDURE NURSING INSTRUCTIONS

Cleanse the skin at the surgical site with sterile saline to wash away dried blood. The patient can hold gauze over the site for 10 minutes. Antibiotic cream and a gauze pressure dressing should then be taped over the wound. The patient should immediately wear a firm, supportive bra. The gauze can be removed the next day.

Disposable needles and suture needles are disposed of in a proper sharps container.

Soiled gauze is disposed of in an appropriate biohazard waste container.

The instruments are scrubbed, washed, rinsed, and dried. The surgical instruments should be sterilized in the autoclave.

PROCEDURE RECORDING FORM

Simple Open Breast Biopsy

PATIENT NAME: ______________________________

AGE: ______________

DATE: ______________

Indication for the procedure: ______________

Lesion location:

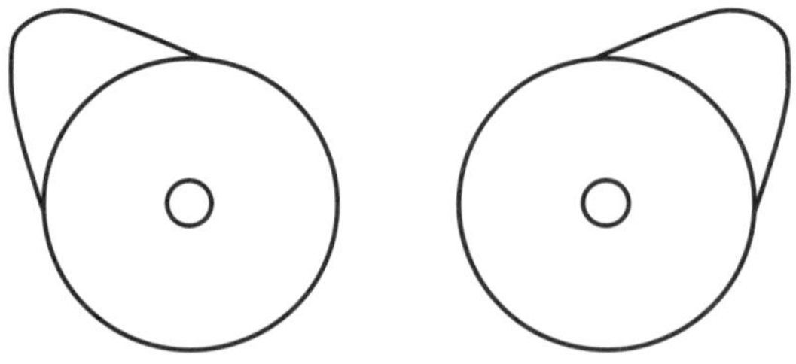

Diameter size: ______________
Date of most recent mammogram: ______________
Finding: ______________
Most recent needle biopsy date: ______________
Finding: ______________

Circle the Correct Response:

Pain at the site?	Yes	No	Axillary nodes?	Yes	No
Prior surgical biopsy?	Yes	No	Skin dimpling?	Yes	No
Smooth-walled lesion?	Yes	No	Rock-hard mass?	Yes	No
Mass fixed to chest wall?	Yes	No	Prior cysts?	Yes	No
Breast Ca in 1st-degree rel.?	Yes	No	Nipple discharge?	Yes	No

Procedure Description:

The patient lay supine. The skin over the lesion was marked with a skin marking pen, and a circumferential incision was designed. The skin and subcutaneous tissues were anesthetized with 2% lidocaine with epinephrine. Additional anesthetic was then placed into the breast tissue surrounding the lesion. Skin incision was made with a No. 15 blade. The incision was carried down into the subcutaneous tissue. The lesion was palpated and grasped with an Allis clamp. Incision was carried out around the lesion, removing a rim of normal breast tissue on all sides. Bleeding sites were clamped with a hemostat, and additional anesthetic was administered. Once the lesion was completely removed, the wound was palpated and the remaining tissue was felt to be normal. The hemostats were removed, and cautery was applied to bleeding sites. Figure-of-8, 4-0 Vicryl sutures were used on persisting or vigorous bleeding sites. The wound was dry at closure. The breast tissue was not closed. The subcutaneous tissue was closed with a running 5-0 Vicryl subcutaneous suture, and adhesive tape was applied to the skin. The wound was dry, and pressure bandage was applied. The patient tolerated the procedure well. Specimen orientation: Nylon suture in the anterior (skin) surface, Vicryl cut with long ends at 12 o'clock (cephalad surface), and Vicryl cut with short ends at 3 o'clock (lateral surface).

Other marking for orientation: ______________
Complications: ______________
Estimated blood loss: ______________ Figure-of-8 sutures for bleeding? Yes No
Impression:

Plan:

Physician: ______________
CC: ______________

CHAPTER 8

Punch Biopsy of the Skin

PATIENT INFORMATION

Punch Biopsy of the Skin

What is punch biopsy?

Punch biopsy is a commonly performed diagnostic procedure on abnormal skin growths or skin tumors. It is performed using a local anesthetic (numbing medicine). A pencil-like instrument is used to remove a small, thin cylinder of tissue. The small hole in the skin then is sutured (stitched) closed.

What happens to the biopsy specimen once it is removed?

After removal, the biopsy specimen is sent to the hospital laboratory for further evaluation. The skin is examined under the microscope by a specialist physician known as a pathologist. The pathologist is trained to correctly identify the cells of various skin growths, which will assist your doctor in selecting the proper treatment.

Are there any complications after punch biopsy?

Complications are very uncommon following this simple procedure, but can occur with any surgical procedure. Some of the complications associated with punch biopsy include local bleeding and bruising, pain, infection, allergic reaction to the numbing medicine used in the procedure, or damage to the structures beneath the skin site (such as an artery or a nerve). Your doctor will take care to reduce the likelihood of these rare problems.

What happens to the site where the piece of skin was removed?

The biopsy site is usually sutured (stitched) closed, and the area often heals with a very small scar. Your doctor may ask you to return in 5 to 14 days for removal of the skin stitches. You will be given instructions on how to help the biopsy site heal. The results of the biopsy evaluation will determine if further treatment of the skin site will be needed.

How long before I will receive the results of the biopsy evaluation?

The biopsy results usually are available in 1 to 2 weeks. Your doctor's office will notify you of the results. You do not need to call the office in the first 2 weeks after the procedure. Sometimes the doctor will review the results with you at the follow-up (suture removal) visit. If 1 month goes by and you have not heard from your doctor, call the office for the results of the biopsy.

PATIENT INSTRUCTIONS

Following Punch Biopsy of the Skin

1. Immediately after removal of the skin biopsy and closure of the biopsy site, your doctor will apply antibiotic ointment and a Band-Aid to the site. Continue to apply antibiotic ointment daily to the wound until it is completely healed. The antibiotic ointment Mycitracin Plus is recommended because it contains numbing medicine in addition to the antibiotic.

2. You can remove the Band-Aid at any time, but you may prefer to keep the wound covered. Keeping the site covered with a Band-Aid may prevent rubbing at the site and will also keep the antibiotic ointment off your clothing.

3. If the biopsy site begins to bleed, apply direct pressure for 10 minutes. If it continues to bleed, please call your doctor.

4. If you experience discomfort at the biopsy site, you can take ibuprofen (brand names: Advil, Motrin, Nuprin), three 200-mg tablets three times a day with food, or acetaminophen (brand name: Tylenol), two 325-mg tablets every 6 hours.

5. Skin infection can follow any surgical procedure. If you develop increased pain, redness, pus, or swelling at the surgery site, call your doctor.

6. Your doctor will notify you of the time for suture (stitch) removal, usually about 1 week following the procedure. Sometimes a single stitch that is used to close a punch biopsy site falls out on its own. If the stitch falls out and the wound is not gapping open, you can call and cancel your follow-up visit.

7. Most doctors use the suture removal visit to discuss the pathology results of the biopsy. The results generally take about 1 to 2 weeks to return. The doctor's office will contact you with the results. You do not need to call in the first 2 weeks. If 1 month goes by and you have not heard from your doctor's office, call to check on the biopsy results.

This handout provides a general overview on this subject and may not apply to everyone. Talk to your family doctor to find out if this information applies to you and to get more information.

INFORMED CONSENT FORM

Punch Biopsy of the Skin

PATIENT: ______________________________

DATE: ____________________

1. I hereby authorize Dr. ____________________ to perform the procedure known as punch biopsy of the skin.

2. I understand that punch biopsy is a surgical procedure performed following the administration of local anesthesia. I understand that a small piece of skin or a portion of a skin growth will be removed for further examination under the microscope. While punch biopsy can completely remove a very small growth, generally this procedure does not completely remove larger lesions. I understand that punch biopsy usually produces a minimal scar. I understand that the practice of medicine is not an exact science, and that no guarantee can be made regarding the outcome of my planned procedure.

3. My doctor has explained to me that this procedure generally is safe, but that certain risks accompany any surgical procedure. Risks associated with punch biopsy of the skin include:

Local bleeding and bruising in the surrounding tissues

Pain associated with the surgery or the healing process

Excessive scarring at the surgery site

Allergic reaction to the numbing medicine or the surgical instruments

Local infection in the surrounding tissues

Damage to structures beneath the skin such as an artery or nerve

Rare, unusual reactions, including possible death following any surgical procedure

4. I understand that there are alternatives to this procedure, including shave biopsy of the skin, lesion removal by fusiform excision technique, or no excision at all. I understand that the other techniques may not provide the same advantages as the punch biopsy technique. I understand that I can refuse this procedure.

5. I understand that unforeseen conditions may alter the planned procedure. I give permission to my doctor to alter the procedure (such as to change the punch biopsy to fusiform excisional biopsy), if necessary, or to administer additional anesthetics or other medications if I should need them for the completion of my procedure.

6. I have read this form and the other sheets given to me by my physician. I have had my questions answered to my satisfaction.

WITNESS: ______________________

PATIENT: ______________________

DATE: ______________________

MINOR: ______________________

PARENT: ______________________

NURSING INSTRUCTIONS

Punch Biopsy of the Skin

NONSTERILE TRAY FOR ANESTHESIA

Place the following items on a nonsterile sheet covering a Mayo stand:

- Nonsterile gloves
- 1 inch of 4 × 4 gauze soaked with povidone-iodine solution
- 3-mL syringe filled with 2% lidocaine with epinephrine (Xylocaine with Epinephrine)
- 30-gauge needle
- Labeled formalin container(s) for the number of biopsies to be performed

STERILE TRAY FOR THE PROCEDURE

Place the following items on a sterile sheet covering a Mayo stand:

- Sterile gloves (Some physicians choose to perform the procedure using the nonsterile gloves used for anesthesia.)
- Desired punch biopsy instrument (3 or 4 mm)
- Needle holder for suturing
- Desired size suture (4-0, 5-0, or 6-0 nylon suture depending on body site)
- Iris scissors
- 21-gauge, 1 1/4-inch needle for elevating the specimen (Alternately, the nonsterile anesthesia needle can be used.)
- Sterile fenestrated drape (Some physicians choose to perform the procedure without a covering drape.)

POSTPROCEDURE NURSING INSTRUCTIONS

Cleanse the area with saline or water if blood or povidone-iodine solution remain on the skin following the procedure. Apply antibiotic ointment and a bandage to the site. The patient can apply pressure to the site if any bleeding is noted.

The anesthesia needles, suture needles, and disposable punch biopsy instrument are disposed of in an appropriate sharps container.

The bloody gauze is disposed of in an appropriate biohazard waste container.

The instruments are scrubbed, washed, rinsed, and dried. The instruments are placed in a clear sterilization packet, either individually or as a surgical tray, and sterilized in the autoclave.

PROCEDURE RECORDING FORM

Punch Biopsy of the Skin

PATIENT NAME: ____________________

DATE: ____________________

AGE: ____________________

MEDICATIONS: ____________________

Lesion 1

Site: ____________________ Drawing of the site:
Indication: ____________________

Clinical impression: ____________________
Punch biopsy instrument: ____ mm
Suture closure: ____ -0 Nylon

Lesion 2

Site: ____________________ Drawing of the site:
Indication: ____________________

Clinical impression: ____________________
Punch biopsy instrument: ____ mm
Suture closure: ____ -0 Nylon

Lesion 3

Site: ____________________ Drawing of the site:
Indication: ____________________

Clinical impression: ____________________
Punch biopsy instrument: ____ mm
Suture closure: ____ -0 Nylon

Procedure Description: The patient gave informed consent for the procedure. The biopsy site was selected, the skin was cleansed with povidone-iodine solution, and the area was anesthetized with 2% lidocaine with epinephrine and a 30-gauge needle. The desired size punch biopsy instrument was selected, and the instrument was held vertically over the skin. The instrument was rotated downward until the entire skin thickness was penetrated. The punch instrument was removed, and the cylinder of skin was elevated using the anesthesia needle. Iris scissors were used to cut free the skin specimen from the subcutaneous tissue. The specimen was placed in formalin, and the site was closed using nylon suture. Good hemostasis was observed. Antibiotic ointment was placed over the wound, and a bandage was applied.

Complications: ____________________

Plan: Suture removal in ____ days.
Patient to be notified of the pathology results.
Wound instructions given.
Postprocedure instruction sheet given to patient.

Physician: ____________________
CC: ____________________

SECTION II

THERAPEUTIC PROCEDURES

CHAPTER 9

Bartholin's Cyst/Abscess Marsupialization

PATIENT INFORMATION

Bartholin's Cyst

What are Bartholin's glands?

Bartholin's glands are two rounded, pea-sized glands at the entrance to the vagina. Normally you don't notice or feel these glands. They lubricate the external skin and the tissues near the entrance of the vagina, but they are not required for vaginal lubrication during sex (intercourse).

Why do the Bartholin's glands enlarge?

If the duct draining the Bartholin's gland becomes blocked, the fluid produced in the gland will make it swell (enlarge). About 2% of all women in the United States develop enlargement in one or both glands. Obstruction of the glands usually results from tissue irritation, inflammation, or injury. A cyst may develop, and infection or an abscess may occur.

How do I know if an infection develops?

Women with an infection in the enlarged gland usually complain of pain with sitting or walking. The tissues at the entrance to the vagina may become swollen and tender and may bleed. The abscess may drain on its own by the third or fourth day, but most women seek help before that time. Sex is usually impossible once the infection develops.

Do Bartholin's cysts need to be treated?

Cysts that are not causing pain or other symptoms may not need treatment. You may be advised to take warm sitz baths to try to make the cyst or early abscess disappear. If you have an infection, you may be given antibiotics. Because of the slight risk of cancerous cysts in women over age 40, cysts are sometimes removed in these women.

What are the surgical treatments?

Painful cysts or abscesses can be treated surgically. One option is to open the enlarged gland and drain it, but the swelling can come back with this procedure. Another option is to remove the entire gland, but this is an extensive and difficult procedure with frequent bleeding complications. Another choice is to open the gland and insert a special balloon for 4 to 6 weeks, creating a scar tract that prevents the gland duct from blocking again. However, some women do not like having the balloon in the wound, and do not like having to refrain from sex for that length of time. So, instead, many doctors prefer marsupialization. In marsupialization, the top of the gland is removed, and the skin edges are sutured (stitched) to the walls of the gland. As this wound heals, the gland shrinks and the duct is forced to remain open.

What complications can develop after this procedure?

Bleeding may develop after all surgical procedures, including simple incision and drainage. Localized infection may occur, and rarely can develop in the bloodstream after surgery on abscesses. Scarring and chronic pain in the tissues also have been rarely reported as complications after the surgical procedure.

This handout provides a general overview on this subject and may not apply to everyone. Talk to your family doctor to find out if this information applies to you and to get more information.

PATIENT INSTRUCTIONS

Following Bartholin's Cyst Marsupialization

1. After your procedure, you should not shave the area, use powders or perfumes or douches, or perform other activities that may irritate the tissues until they are completely healed. Antibiotic cream should be applied to the wound twice daily until it heals (about 2 weeks). The antibiotic cream Mycitracin Plus is useful because it contains numbing medication in addition to the antibiotic.

2. A large amount of gauze has been placed against the wound to absorb any persisting drainage or blood. Please apply direct pressure with your hand over the gauze for 1 to 2 hours after the surgery. If your gauze becomes soaked in blood, you should reapply dry gauze. If you notice bleeding in the first 2 days after the surgery, apply direct pressure again for 1 hour. If the bleeding will not stop, or is excessive, please call your doctor. You can stop placing gauze next to the wound (in your underwear) once the drainage has stopped.

3. The numbing medicine used during the surgery should begin to wear off about 1 hour after the procedure. You should take ibuprofen (brand names: Advil, Motrin, Nuprin), three or four 200-mg tablets three times a day with food, for any pain noted in the first few days after the surgery. You can add acetaminophen (brand name: Tylenol), two 325-mg tablets every 6 hours, to the ibuprofen if you need added pain control.

4. Please refrain from sex (intercourse), bicycling, rowing, horseback riding, or any other bouncing or strenuous activities for 10 days after the surgery. You may walk, sit, and return to work the day after the procedure if you are comfortable. Sexual intercourse may be resumed after 10 days, when the tenderness is gone.

5. Infection can develop after the procedure, or rarely can spread to other body sites after the surgery. If you develop increased pain, redness, pus, or swelling at the surgical site, contact your doctor (even if you are taking antibiotics). Call your doctor if you develop weakness, chills, fever, or dizziness.

6. The surgical site may feel strange or slightly uncomfortable for a few weeks. Some patients are concerned about a firm scar they feel at the surgical site. If you remain concerned about the site, please return to allow your doctor to re-examine you. The scar often shrinks and becomes less noticeable over time. The cyst may come back, but this is not likely. If you think you are developing another cyst or a cyst on the opposite side, please return to the doctor's office.

INFORMED CONSENT FORM

Bartholin's Cyst Marsupialization

PATIENT: ______________________________

DATE: ____________________

1. I hereby authorize Dr. ____________________ to perform the procedure known as marsupialization of an enlarged Bartholin's cyst.

2. I understand that this is a procedure performed under local anesthesia on the tissues in my vaginal area. I understand that this procedure will attempt to drain the enlarged gland that is causing my discomfort. The surgery will attempt to reform an opening to the gland so the gland can continue to function. It is also hoped that the gland will not close again, reforming another cyst. I understand that the practice of medicine is not an exact science, and that no guarantee can be made regarding the outcome of my planned procedure.

3. My doctor has explained to me that this procedure is generally safe, but that certain risks accompany any surgical procedure. Risks associated with the marsupialization procedure include:
    - Bleeding, sometimes requiring transfusion or hospitalization
    - Pain associated with the surgery or the healing process
    - Excessive scarring after the surgery
    - Allergic reaction to the numbing medication or surgical instruments
    - Localized infection in the tissues near the vagina
    - Infection that spreads throughout the body
    - Rare, unusual reactions, including possible death following any surgical procedure

4. I understand that there are alternatives to this procedure, including simple incision and drainage of the cyst, complete removal of the cyst, management with antibiotics and warm soaks, or no treatment at all. I understand that I can refuse this procedure.

5. I understand that unforeseen conditions may alter the planned procedure. I give permission to my doctor to alter the procedure (such as to remove the entire gland or biopsy a tumorous growth) if necessary, or to administer additional anesthetics or other medication if I should need them for the completion of my procedure.

6. I have read this form and other sheets given to me by my physician. I have had my questions answered to my satisfaction.

WITNESS: ______________________

PATIENT: ______________________

DATE: ______________________

MINOR: ______________________

PARENT: ______________________

NURSING INSTRUCTIONS

Bartholin's Cyst Marsupialization

PATIENT PREPARATION

The patient is asked to undress from the waist down and is given a gown. An absorbent sheet is placed beneath the patient. The patient can be left seated on the table to speak with the physician. The patient is placed in the lithotomy position for the procedure.

NONSTERILE TRAY FOR ANESTHESIA

Nonsterile gloves and mask

4 × 4 gauze

Povidone-iodine solution

2 10-mL syringes with 27-gauge 1 1/4-inch needles filled with 2% lidocaine with epinephrine (Xylocaine with Epinephrine)

STERILE TRAY FOR THE PROCEDURE

Place the following items on a sterile drape covering the Mayo stand:

- Sterile gloves
- 3 hemostats (mosquito clamps)
- No. 15 blade and blade handle (No. 11 blade can be used alternately)
- Needle holder
- 3-0 Vicryl suture
- 2 inches of 4 × 4 gauze
- Mayo or tissue scissors
- Iris scissors (for cutting sutures)
- Adson forceps with teeth
- 2 Allis forceps for holding tissue edges
- Sterile battery cautery (Can reuse the disposable units if the tip is cleaned and disinfected in glutaraldehyde [Cidex], and the unit is slipped into a sterile glove that is on the surgery tray allowing only the instrument tip to protrude through the tip of one of the fingers on the glove.)

POSTPROCEDURE NURSING INSTRUCTIONS

Cleanse the area with sterile saline or water on gauze to wash away the dried blood. Antibiotic cream can be applied to the surgical site, and 1 inch of 4 × 4 gauze can be placed over the site. Ask the patient to apply direct pressure over the gauze. The gauze can be held over the surgical site with the patient's underwear.

Anesthesia needles and suture needles should be disposed of in appropriate sharps containers.

The instruments should be scrubbed, washed, rinsed, and dried. Place the instruments in a clear sterilization packet, either individually or as a surgical tray, and sterilize in the autoclave.

Bloody gauze should be disposed of in appropriate biohazard waste container.

PROCEDURE RECORDING FORM

Bartholin's Cyst Marsupialization

PATIENT NAME: ______________________________

DATE: ______________

AGE: ______________

How long have symptoms been present? ______________

Circle the Correct Response:

Pain?	Yes	No	Discharge?	Yes	No
Drainage?	Yes	No	Prior STDs?	Yes	No
Bleeding?	Yes	No	Dyspareunia?	Yes	No
Swelling?	Yes	No	HIV positive?	Yes	No

Date of the last Pap smear: ______________ Result: ______________

Side affected: R L Diameter size of the lesion: ______________

Procedure Description: The patient gave informed consent for the procedure. Other options were discussed, and the patient elected to undergo the marsupialization procedure. The patient was placed in the lithotomy position, and the labial area cleansed with povidone-iodine solution. The area above and around the cyst was anesthetized with 2% lidocaine with epinephrine. Sterile drapes were placed over the area. The cyst was lifted forward and stabilized using a nondominant hand. A vertical fusiform (elliptical) incision was made at the mucocutaneous junction over the cyst using a No. 15 blade. Bleeding areas were clamped with hemostats and cauterized. The incision was then carried into the cyst, and the cyst contents drained. The fusiform island of tissue, including the roof of the cyst, was cut free using scissors. The cyst wall was palpated, septae were broken up with blunt dissection, and no nodular areas were noted on the cyst walls. The edges of the cyst wall were pinched upward and sutured to the overlying skin using interrupted 3-0 or 4-0 Vicryl sutures. Good hemostasis was achieved. Antibiotic cream was applied to the wound, and gauze was applied over the site. The patient tolerated the procedure well.

GC culture obtained?	Yes	No	Routine culture obtained?	Yes	No
Iodoform gauze packing?	Yes	No	Biopsy obtained?	Yes	No

Complications: ______________________________

Diagnosis:

Plan:

Postprocedure instruction sheet given? Yes No

Physician: ______________

CC: ______________

CHAPTER 10

Eyelid Chalazia

PATIENT INFORMATION

Eyelid Chalazia

What is a chalazion?

A chalazion is a hard, usually painless bump on the eyelid that results from chronic inflammation of the meibomian glands of the eyelids. When a chalazion first develops, it can become infected and appear red, swollen, and tender. Frequently, it will go away on its own or with minimal treatment. However, some persist as hard, less inflamed bumps. Chronic chalazia (more than one chalazion are called chalazia) can be irritating with eye movement, can become uncomfortable, or can be unattractive.

Are chalazia associated with skin disease?

Yes. Chalazia are associated with skin disorders such as seborrheic dermatitis, chronic blepharitis, and rosacea. These skin problems can cause chronic inflammation of the eyelid tissues, resulting in blockage of the meibomian glands. People who have one of these skin problems often experience many cysts in different sites on the eyelids over many years.

How are chalazia treated?

Acute chalazia are treated with warm compresses (a washcloth soaked in warm water) held to the eyelid for 10 minutes at a time, four times a day. Antibiotic eye drops or ointment also may be helpful for an early, inflamed chalazion. Some chalazia go away with time. However, if the chalazia persist (chronic chalazia), antibiotics are no longer effective. A chalazion can be injected with a small amount of steroid medicine, although skin thinning, bruising, or blood clots can result from this treatment. Surgical treatment is generally prescribed for chronic chalazia.

What happens during the surgical treatment?

The procedure is performed in your doctor's office. The eye is anesthetized (numbed) with several drops of medicine. A plastic shield is gently placed over the eyeball to protect your eye. The eyelid must be injected with a local anesthetic. A tiny needle is used to administer the medicine very slowly, but this can be uncomfortable. It is important that you do not move during the injection. Once the eyelid is numb, the chalazion is opened with a tiny incision (cut), either from the inside or the outside of the eyelid. The jellylike contents of the chalazion are removed. A small curette (an instrument that looks like a tiny ice cream scoop) is placed inside the chalazion, and the walls are scraped so it will scar closed.

What complications can occur after the procedure?

The eye can be injured during the procedure, but this is rare, and efforts are made to prevent injury. Chalazia that are very close to the tear duct that drains tears from the eye can produce damage to the drainage system. Infections are very unusual, but can occur. The procedure can rarely produce a noticeable scar on the eyelid, despite the use of tiny incisions. A chalazion can come back after removal, or a new chalazion can develop next to where the old one was removed. Rarely, a cancerous growth may be discovered next to a chalazia. If it seems that you do not have a typical cyst, the tumor may be removed so it can be studied further (a biopsy).

This handout provides a general overview on this subject and may not apply to everyone. Talk to your family doctor to find out if this information applies to you and to get more information.

PATIENT INSTRUCTIONS

Following Chalazion Removal

1. Your doctor will ask you to apply gentle direct pressure to your eyelid after the procedure. Hold clean gauze to the surgical site for 10 minutes in the office and for 30 minutes after you leave.

2. Your doctor will place an antibiotic drop in your eye after the procedure. You should not need to apply any medicine to your eye at home.

3. Bruising of the eyelid commonly occurs after this procedure. Don't be alarmed if you develop a "black eye" after the surgery. However, if your eyelid is swelling, and the bruising is increasing, immediately apply direct pressure. If the swelling continues to increase, call your doctor.

4. If you develop bleeding from your incision, apply direct pressure. If you cannot stop the bleeding, call your doctor.

5. Avoid rubbing your eye for at least 3 days after your procedure. Rubbing the eyelid often causes swelling. If you find it difficult to keep your hands away from your eye when you are in bed, consider wearing clean, heavy gloves, mittens, or socks over your hands.

6. If you feel any discomfort after your surgery, you can take acetaminophen (brand name: Tylenol), two 325-mg tablets every 4 hours, or ibuprofen (brand names: Advil, Motrin, Nuprin), two to four 200-mg tablets three times a day with food. Please call your doctor if you note any infection, drainage, redness, excessive pain, or significant swelling during the first week after your surgery.

7. Your doctor may want to reexamine your eyelid in 1 month. Some patients develop other chalazia, so contact your doctor if any additional bumps develop on your eyelid.

8. Good hygiene on the eyelids may help prevent future chalazia. Two weeks after your surgery, you can begin to gently wash the eyelids with warm water every day, using a washcloth in the shower, to help prevent debris from accumulating on the edge of the eyelid.

INFORMED CONSENT FORM

Chalazion Removal

PATIENT: ____

DATE: ________________________

1. I hereby authorize Dr. ____________________ to perform the procedure known as chalazion removal.

2. I understand that this procedure is performed with local anesthesia injected into the tissues around my eye. I understand that this procedure will attempt to drain the cyst in my eyelid, scrape the walls of the cyst, and have the cyst scar closed. It is hoped that another cyst will not form at the same site or nearby, but I understand that recurrences are common. I also understand that the practice of medicine is not an exact science, and that no guarantee can be made regarding the outcome of my planned procedure.

3. My doctor has explained to me that this procedure is generally safe, but that certain risks accompany any surgical procedure. Risks associated with the chalazion removal procedure include:

Injury to the eye, despite efforts to shield the eye

Bleeding from the eyelid, sometimes requiring cauterization

Excessive scarring on the eyelid after the surgery

Pain associated with the surgery or the healing process

Allergic reaction to the numbing medication or the surgical tools

Localized infection in the eyelid or around the eye

Rare, unusual reactions, including possible death following any surgical procedure

4. I understand that there are alternatives to this procedure, including simple incision and drainage of the cyst, removal of the cyst, injection of corticosteroid medication into the cyst, or no treatment at all. I understand that I can refuse this procedure.

5. I understand that unforeseen conditions may alter the planned procedure. I give permission to my doctor to alter the planned procedure (such as to perform electrosurgical cautery) if necessary, or to administer additional anesthetics or other medication if I should need them for the completion of my procedure. I also understand that rarely cancer may appear to be a chalazion, and that if the surgery discovers that my lesion is not a typical cyst, my doctor may ask for the opportunity to completely remove the tumor.

6. I have read this form and other sheets given to me by my physician. I have had my questions answered to my satisfaction.

WITNESS: ____________________________

PATIENT: ____________________________

DATE: ____________________________

MINOR: ____________________________

PARENT: ____________________________

NURSING INSTRUCTIONS

Chalazia Removal

PATIENT PREPARATION

The patient is placed in supine position. An absorbent sheet is draped inside the patient's collar and over the upper chest. Several tissues are placed in the patient's hand for any solutions that may drain from the eye before or after the surgery.

NONSTERILE TRAY FOR THE PROCEDURE

Place the following items on a nonsterile drape on the Mayo stand:

- Nonsterile gloves and mask
- 3-mL syringe filled with 1% lidocaine (Xylocaine); 30-gauge needle
- Fine-tipped Adson forceps without teeth
- Iris scissors
- Sterile 2-mm chalazion curette
- Sterile 3-mm chalazion curette
- 1 chalazion clamp
- Sterile No. 11 blade
- 1 inch of 4 × 4 gauze
- Refrigerated bottle of proparacaine 0.5% ophthalmic solution (Ophthetic)
- 1 bottle of saline eye wash
- Tobramycin (Tobrex) ophthalmic ointment
- 6 small cotton-tipped applicators
- Gentamicin (Garamycin) or ciprofloxacin (Ciloxan) ophthalmic solution
- 1 adult eye shield with a small swirl of tobramyein ointment inside the shield
- Suction cup applicator for the eye shield

POSTPROCEDURE NURSING INSTRUCTIONS

The patient should be given some 4 × 4 gauze and instructed to hold pressure to the site for 10 minutes immediately after the surgery.

Blood clots inside the eye can be washed away with saline eye wash, but often this is not necessary. Garamycin or ciprofloxacin ophthalmic solution (two drops) should be placed inside the lower eyelid after the procedure.

The metal surgical instruments should be scrubbed, washed, rinsed, and dried. The instruments should be placed in clear sterilization packets and sterilized in the autoclave.

The plastic eye shields should be washed, rinsed, and placed in glutaraldehyde. After the disinfection, the shield is rinsed with sterile saline. A small swirl of tobramycin ophthalmic ointment is smeared on the shield before it is stored in its container.

Bloody gauze is disposed of in an appropriate biohazard waste container.

Proparacaine solution is stored in the refrigerator.

PROCEDURE RECORDING FORM

Chalazion Removal

PATIENT NAME: ______________________________

AGE: ______________

DATE: ______________

History of prior chalazia? ______________
Prior treatments: ______________
Skin conditions: Rosacea Seborrheic dermatitis Chronic blepharitis Other: ______________
Affected Eye(s):

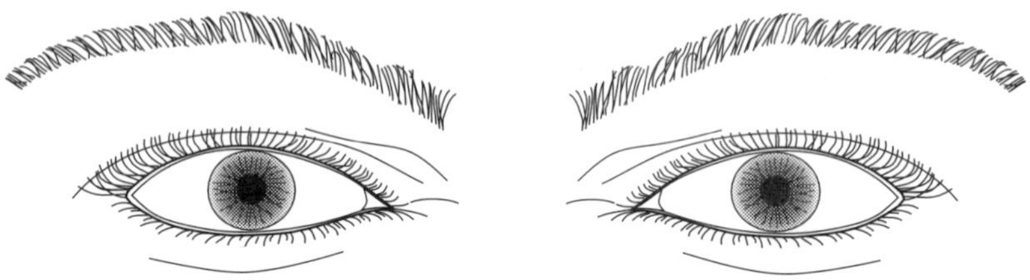

Procedure Description: The eye was anesthetized with several drops of proparacaine 0.5% ophthalmic solution. The eye shield, coated with tobramycin ophthalmic ointment, was gently slipped over the globe, and several drops of proparacaine was reapplied. The affected eyelid was anesthetized with 1% xylocaine. The chalazion clamp was placed, and the chalazion entered with a No. 11 blade. The 2-mm or 3-mm chalazion curette was used to remove the gelatinous contents. The curette was used to vigorously scrape the sides of the chalazion. The clamp was removed, pressure was applied for hemostasis, and blood was irrigated from the eye. The eye was treated with garamycin or ciprofloxacin ophthalmic drops. The patient held gentle pressure to the site with gauze for 10 minutes after the procedure.

Chalazion curette used: 2 mm ____ 3 mm ____
Patient tolerance: ______________________________
Complications: ______________________________
Impression: Chalazion
 Number treated and location: ______________
Plan:
 Apply direct pressure for at least 10 minutes after the procedure.
 Reapply direct pressure if bleeding recurs.
 Call if any signs of infection such as swelling, redness, or pus.
 Patient to take ibuprofen or acetaminophen for discomfort.
 Patient reminded of the recurrent nature of chalazia.
 Postprocedure instruction sheet given.

Patient informed: Yes No
Received postprocedure instruction sheet: Yes No

Physician: ______________
CC: ______________

CHAPTER 11

Minimal Excision Technique for Removal of an Epidermoid (Sebaceous) Cyst

PATIENT INFORMATION

Minimal Excision Technique for Removal of an Epidermoid Cyst

What is an epidermoid cyst?

An epidermoid cyst is a benign (not cancer), slow-growing skin growth that results from injury to a hair follicle in association with acne, from a defect in the skin, or from injury to the skin beneath the skin surface. The cysts contain a cheesy, yellow material. Rupture of the cyst can release some of the cheesy material into the skin, resulting in a reaction that produces redness, tenderness, and swelling.

Where are epidermoid cysts commonly found on the body?

Epidermoid cysts commonly appear on acne-prone areas of the face, neck, and upper trunk. Cysts may also be found on the scrotum, behind the ears, and on the scalp. Epidermoid cysts are rarely found on the fingers, palms of the hands, and soles of the feet. Miniature epidermoid cysts (called milia) can develop in skin that is injured or scraped.

Are there any problems or complications associated with epidermoid cysts?

Ruptured cysts can cause skin scarring and discomfort. Cysts can rarely develop an associated skin cancer. Epidermoid cysts are often a cosmetic problem or are a cause of embarrassment for people. One of the major problems comes from growths that appear to be benign epidermoid cysts, but are actually more aggressive skin tumors.

What is the minimal excision technique?

This simple, effective surgical procedure removes the cyst wall and the cheesy material inside the cyst. If the entire cyst wall is removed, the chance of the cyst coming back is low. A tiny cut is made in the skin following the administration of local anesthesia (numbing medicine), the cyst contents are vigorously squeezed out, and the cyst wall is pulled through the tiny skin opening. The skin opening is so small that sutures (stitches) are often not needed to close the wound.

Is the minimal excision technique always successful in removing the cyst wall?

The doctor may not be able to pull the cyst wall through the small skin incision. Cysts that have been inflamed or previously ruptured may have extensive scarring around the cyst wall and be more difficult to remove. If the cyst wall can't be removed, your doctor will perform a standard excision (a larger surgical procedure) to remove it.

PATIENT INSTRUCTIONS

Following Minimal Excision of an Epidermoid Cyst

1. Your doctor will ask you to use your hand to hold direct, firm pressure on the site for 1 to 2 hours after the procedure. Because no deep stitches are placed in the wound, it is important that pressure be applied to avoid blood from collecting where the cyst was.

2. Antibiotic ointment will be applied to the wound immediately after the procedure. Antibiotic ointment should be applied daily, until the wound is completely healed.

3. Some gauze may be taped over the surgery site, unless the cyst was on your scalp. If the gauze becomes soaked with blood, apply firm pressure over the area and change the gauze. If the bleeding continues despite the pressure, please call your doctor. The gauze can be removed the morning following your procedure, and the site can be covered with a Band-Aid.

4. Some wounds will have a clear or yellow fluid drainage after this procedure. The drainage is fairly common after the removal of large cysts. This drainage usually stops within 1 week after the surgery. If pus drainage is noted, especially if the wound is red or tender, call your doctor.

5. You can take a shower 36 hours after the procedure. You can take a bath once the wound has completely healed. Do not bathe or swim while the wound remains open, or if fluid drainage is noted. Vigorous physical activity can be resumed 1 week following your procedure.

6. Occasionally, a small piece of cyst wall may remain beneath the skin, and the cyst can reform. If you notice a lump or cyst at, or near, the original surgical site, return to be examined by your doctor.

7. If stitches are used to close your wound, you will be asked to return to have them removed in 7 to 10 days.

8. Report any problems, such as infection or bleeding, to your doctor.

INFORMED CONSENT FORM

Epidermoid Cyst Removal

PATIENT: ____________________________________

DATE ______________________

1. I hereby authorize Dr. __________________ to perform the procedure known as removal of an epidermoid (sebaceous) cyst.

2. I understand that this is a procedure performed under local anesthesia. I understand that my physician may attempt the removal of the unwanted skin cyst through a small incision. If the cyst is scarred, it may require the standard removal technique through a larger incision. I understand that my physician will attempt to remove the entire wall of the cyst so that it does not recur. I understand that the practice of medicine is not an exact science, and that no guarantee can be made regarding the outcome of my planned procedure.

3. My doctor has explained to me that this procedure is generally safe, but that certain risks accompany any surgical procedure. Risks associated with epidermoid cyst removal include:
   - Bleeding and bruising in the surrounding tissues
   - Pain associated with the procedure or the healing process
   - Excessive scarring associated with the procedure
   - Allergic reaction to the numbing medication or the surgical instruments
   - Localized infection in the surrounding tissues
   - Damage to the structures below the skin, such as a nerve or blood vessel
   - Rare, unusual reactions, including possible death following any surgical procedure

4. I understand that there are alternatives to this procedure, including simple incision and drainage, placement of iodine crystals into the cyst, electrosurgical or laser destruction, or freezing (cryosurgery) of the cyst. I understand that I can refuse the surgical removal procedure.

5. I understand that unforeseen conditions may alter the planned procedure. I give permission to my doctor to alter the procedure (such as switching to the standard removal technique using a larger incision), if necessary, or to administer additional anesthetics or other medications if I should need them for the completion of my procedure.

6. I have read this form and other sheets given to me by my physician. I have had my questions answered to my satisfaction.

WITNESS: __________________________

PATIENT: __________________________

DATE: ____________________________

MINOR: ___________________________

PARENT: __________________________

NURSING INSTRUCTIONS

Minimal Excision Technique for Epidermoid (Sebaceous) Cyst Removal

NONSTERILE TRAY FOR ANESTHESIA

Place the following items on a nonfenestrated sheet covering a Mayo stand:

- Nonsterile gloves and mask
- 1 inch of 4 × 4 gauze soaked with povidone-iodine solution
- 1 inch of 4 × 4 gauze
- One 5-mL syringe, filled with 2% lidocaine with epinephrine (Xylocaine with Epinephrine), with a 30-gauge needle attached
- 25-gauge, 1 1/4-inch needle (for anesthetizing beneath the cyst)

STERILE TRAY FOR THE PROCEDURE

Place the following items on a sterile disposable sheet covering a Mayo stand:

- Sterile gloves
- Fenestrated disposable drape
- 2 sterile bandages (Band-Aids) to anchor the drape
- 3 small-tipped hemostats (mosquito clamps)
- No. 11 blade
- Needle holder for suturing (if needed)
- Iris scissors
- Adson forceps
- 2 inches of 4 × 4 sterile gauze
- Suture materials (if needed)
- Splatter control shield (if desired)
- Some physicians will use their nonsterile anesthesia gloves for the removal of small or superficial cysts

POSTPROCEDURE NURSING INSTRUCTIONS

The patient or nurse should apply direct pressure to the surgical site with gauze for 10 minutes following the procedure. After this pressure has been applied, the skin can be cleaned with water or sterile saline. The wound can be squeezed to remove any residual blood from beneath the wound.

Antibiotic ointment, 1/2 inch of 4 × 4 gauze, and tape can be applied over the wound. Elastoplast can be applied for additional pressure. If Elastoplast is applied, the edges should be taped down. The pressure bandage can be worn until the morning following the procedure.

All instruments should be brushed, washed, rinsed, and dried. The cleaned instruments are then placed in clear sterilization pouches and are autoclaved, either individually or as a surgical tray.

Sharps (scalpel blade, needles) are disposed of in a proper sharps container.

Bloody gauze is disposed of in a biohazard waste container.

PROCEDURE RECORDING FORM

Minimal Excision Technique for Epidermoid (Sebaceous) Cyst Removal

PATIENT NAME: ______________________________

DATE: ______________

AGE: ______________

How long has the growth been noted? ______________

Symptoms associated with the lesion:

Pain?	Yes	No	Bleeding?	Yes	No
Drainage?	Yes	No	Swelling?	Yes	No
Tenderness?	Yes	No	Irritation?	Yes	No
Itching?	Yes	No	Lesion rubs on clothing?	Yes	No

Side affected: Right Left

Diameter of lesion? ______________

Location of the lesion? ______________

Procedure Description: The patient gave informed consent for the procedure. Other options were discussed, and the patient elected to undergo the minimal excision technique. The skin was washed with povidone-iodine solution, and the skin and subcutaneous tissues anesthetized with 2% lidocaine with epinephrine. The patient tolerated the anesthesia well. A No. 11 blade was used to create a small skin opening into the cyst cavity. The tips of a hemostat were placed into the cyst cavity, widening the opening and assisting with removal of the cyst contents. The tissues surrounding the cyst were squeezed, forcing the cyst contents out onto gauze. Once the entire cyst contents were emptied, and the compression had loosened the cyst wall from surrounding tissues, the hemostat was placed within the cyst cavity and the cyst wall was grasped. The cyst wall was delivered through the incision. The wound was examined for any residual cyst wall. Once the entire wall was removed, pressure was applied over the wound.

Entire cyst wall removed?	Yes	No	Sent to pathology?	Yes	No
Fusiform excision required for complete removal?	Yes	No	Suture used to close the wound?	Yes	No

Suture material: ______________

Complications: ______________________________

Follow-up for wound check: ______________

Follow-up for suture removal: ______________

Impressions:

Epidermoid cyst location: ______________

Plan: Postoperative instructions given.

Pressure to be applied for 2 hours following the procedure.

Bandage to be changed in 24 hours.

Physician: ______________

CC: ______________

CHAPTER 12

Hemorrhoidectomy for Thrombosed External Hemorrhoids

PATIENT INFORMATION

Hemorrhoidectomy for Thrombosed External Hemorrhoids

What are thrombosed hemorrhoids?

All people have blood-filled sacs that cushion the passage of stool through the anal canal. When these sacs become stretched and enlarged, they are called hemorrhoids. Hemorrhoids can occur during or after pregnancy, after long periods in a seated position (such as during long car trips), or because of constipation or diarrhea. Hemorrhoids generally are classified as external hemorrhoids (outside of the anal canal), which can be very painful, and internal hemorrhoids (inside the anal canal), which can protrude and bleed.

External hemorrhoids can become thrombosed (develop blood clots inside) and become very tender. Large blood clots can produce pain with walking, sitting, or passage of stool. It is not clear why healthy people suddenly develop clots in external hemorrhoids.

What treatments are available for thrombosed external hemorrhoids?

The treatments for external hemorrhoids are different from those for internal hemorrhoids. One treatment option is to allow clots in the external hemorrhoids to be slowly absorbed by the body over several weeks. You can try hot baths, ointments or creams for the discomfort. Most experts recommend that the blood clots be surgically removed.

What happens during surgical removal of the thrombosed hemorrhoid?

One procedure creates an incision (cut) over the clot, allowing the doctor to squeeze out the clot. Unfortunately, this quick and easy procedure frequently results in subsequent blood clots reforming and continuing pain. A more extensive procedure (full hemorrhoidectomy) can be performed that removes the clot and the blood vessels in the hemorrhoid. This procedure is longer and may require sutures (stitches) to close the wound, but can yield better results. Local anesthesia (numbing medicine) is used for both procedures.

Does it matter how long my hemorrhoids have hurt?

Surgery on thrombosed external hemorrhoids is best performed in the first 72 hours (3 days) after symptoms start. Significant symptom relief can be achieved with early surgery. After 72 hours, the pain relief from the surgery may not be greater than the discomfort from the surgery itself.

How should I prepare for the procedure?

Come in as soon as the pain develops. No enemas or colon preparation is required. However, you may want to take three or four 200-mg ibuprofen tablets (brand names: Advil, Motrin, Nuprin) before the procedure to lessen discomfort.

PATIENT INSTRUCTIONS

Following Hemorrhoidectomy for Thrombosed External Hemorrhoids

1. You will probably experience some discomfort once the numbing medicine wears off. Pain may be relieved by a combination of taking acetaminophen (brand name: Tylenol), two 325-mg tablets every 4 hours, and ibuprofen (brand names: Advil, Motrin, Nuprin), four 200-mg tablets three times a day. Take the ibuprofen with food to limit stomach upset. Narcotic pain relievers, such as codeine, are not recommended because they can cause constipation, and hard stools can cause tearing in the anus after the procedure.

2. You may have some bloody drainage or mild bleeding with passage of stools for the next few weeks. You can replace clean gauze over the wound, if you desire, whenever the gauze becomes soiled. Even with soft stools, some tearing of the stitches at the surgical site may occur in the first few weeks after the procedure. If you have heavy bleeding, please contact your doctor.

3. Infection is uncommon after this procedure. However, you can apply antibiotic ointment to the site daily for the first week after your surgery. Call your doctor if you develop redness, foul-smelling drainage, swelling, or increasing discomfort in the area.

4. Twenty-minute sitz baths (soaking in a tub of warm water) can be taken in the first few weeks after the procedure to aid in healing and comfort at the site. After 1 week, some people prefer to use medications such as Anusol or Preparation H to soothe the tissues.

5. It is very important that your bowel movements remain soft after surgery. Drink at least six full glasses of water daily. Take over-the-counter (nonprescription) stool softeners such as Colace or Surfak (two capsules two times a day) for at least the first 2 weeks after the procedure.

6. Take a stool-bulking agent such as Metamucil or Citrucel. These products can initially produce gas and bloating, but can be easier to tolerate if the stool softeners are used simultaneously at the start (1 tablespoon daily in a large glass of orange juice, then slowly increase the amount). These agents may prevent colon cancer, and can add to the overall health of your colon.

7. Straining at stool should be avoided after all hemorrhoid treatments. Do not sit for long periods on the toilet. Remove all reading materials from the bathroom. Do not place anything in the rectum, such as an enema, for 3 weeks after the procedure.

8. Your doctor may want to examine your colon for coexisting disease. The procedure is called flexible sigmoidoscopy and it is performed 6 to 12 weeks after your hemorrhoid procedure. You will be given more information if this is scheduled.

This handout provides a general overview on this subject and may not apply to everyone. Talk to your family doctor to find out if this information applies to you and to get more information.

INFORMED CONSENT FORM

Hemorrhoidectomy for Thrombosed External Hemorrhoids

PATIENT: ____________________________

DATE: ________________

1. I hereby authorize Dr. ________________ to perform the procedure known as excision of a thrombosed external hemorrhoid.

2. I understand that this is a procedure performed under local anesthesia on the tissues in my anal area. I understand that the procedure will attempt to remove the blood clot causing my discomfort. The surgery will remove the hemorrhoidal blood vessels that have become clotted, and attempt to prevent further clotting or disease. I understand that the practice of medicine is not an exact science, and that no guarantee can be made regarding the outcome of my planned procedure.

3. My doctor has explained to me that this procedure is generally safe, but that certain risks accompany any surgical procedure. Risks associated with the excision of a thrombosed external hemorrhoid include:
   - Bleeding, sometimes requiring transfusion or hospitalization
   - Pain associated with the surgery or the healing process
   - Excessive scarring or narrowing of the anal canal after the surgery
   - Allergic reaction to the numbing medications or surgical instruments
   - Infection in the anal tissues or throughout the body
   - Damage to the anal muscles, causing inability to control bowel movements
   - Rare, unusual reactions, including possible death following any surgical procedure

4. I understand that there are alternatives to this procedure, including simple incision and drainage of the clot, laser destruction of the tissues, or observation until the clot resolves. I understand that I can refuse this procedure.

5. I understand that unforeseen conditions may alter the planned procedure. I give permission to my doctor to alter the procedure if necessary (such as to cauterize tissues to control bleeding) or to administer additional anesthetics or other medications if I should need them for the completion of my procedure.

6. I have read this form and other sheets given to me by my physician. I have had my questions answered to my satisfaction.

WITNESS: ____________________

PATIENT: ____________________

DATE: ____________________

MINOR: ____________________

PARENT: ____________________

NURSING INSTRUCTIONS

Hemorrhoidectomy for Thrombosed External Hemorrhoids

PATIENT PREPARATION

The patient is asked to undress from the waist down and then is draped. The patient can be left seated on the table to speak with the physician. At the start of the procedure, the patient is rolled onto the left side into the left lateral decubitus position. The knees are bent, and a sheet covers the waist and legs. An absorbent pad is placed under the buttocks and anal area.

NONSTERILE TRAY FOR ANOSCOPY AND ANESTHESIA

Place the following items on a nonsterile drape covering the Mayo stand:

- Nonsterile gloves
- 1 inch of 4 × 4 gauze
- Povidone-iodine solution on 4 × 4 gauze
- 1 inch of 2% lidocaine jelly (Xylocaine) placed on the corner of the drape
- Ives anoscope
- Mask, if desired
- 10-mL syringe filled with 1% lidocaine with a 25-gauge 1 1/4-inch needle attached

STERILE TRAY FOR THE PROCEDURE

Place the following items on a sterile drape covering the Mayo stand:

- Sterile gloves
- 2 inches of sterile 4 × 4 gauze
- 3 hemostats (mosquito clamps)
- No. 15 scalpel blade and blade handle
- Needle holder
- Adson forceps with teeth
- Iris scissors (for cutting sutures)
- Mayo or tissue-cutting scissors
- Allis clamp for holding tissue
- 4-0 Vicryl suture

POSTPROCEDURE NURSING INSTRUCTIONS

The anal area and buttocks can be cleansed with sterile saline or water on gauze to wipe away any blood or drainage from the procedure. Soiled gauze and the absorbent pad are disposed of in an appropriate biohazard waste container.

Antibiotic ointment is applied to the surgical site and 1 inch of clean gauze is placed over the site between the buttocks.

The patient may need assistance with placement of the underwear while maintaining the gauze between the buttocks.

Disposable needles and suture needles are disposed of in appropriate sharps containers.

The instruments should be scrubbed, washed, rinsed, and dried. Place the instruments in a clear sterilization packet, either individually or as a tray, and sterilize in the autoclave.

PROCEDURE RECORDING FORM

Hemorrhoidectomy for Thrombosed External Hemorrhoids

PATIENT NAME: ______________________________

DATE: ______________

AGE: ______________

How long have symptoms been present? ______________

Pain with defecation?	Yes	No
Tenderness?	Yes	No
Pain with sitting?	Yes	No
Discharge?	Yes	No
Bleeding?	Yes	No
Itching?	Yes	No
Prolonged sitting or car rides for work?	Yes	No

Previous problems with hemorrhoids: ______________________________

Previous hemorrhoid surgery: ______________________________

Procedure Description: The patient gave informed consent for the procedure. Alternate procedures were discussed and the patient elected to undergo excision of the thrombosed hemorrhoid. The patient was placed in the left lateral decubitus position. A gloved assistant separated the buttocks and the anal canal was gently inspected for coexisting disease. The area was cleansed with povidone-iodine solution. The base of the hemorrhoid was infiltrated with 1% lidocaine solution. The patient tolerated the anesthesia well. Anoscopy was performed once the patient received the local anesthetic. A fusiform (elliptical) excision was made into the skin overlying the thrombosis. A clamp was placed onto the fusiform island of skin, and traction was applied upward as the hemorrhoidal plexus was sharply excised. Once the thrombosis and hemorrhoidal plexus were excised, the wound base was inspected and any residual clot or hemorrhoidal tissue was removed. Deep, buried 4-0 Vicryl sutures were placed to close the dead space. Good hemostasis was achieved and good wound edge approximation was noted. Antibiotic ointment was applied. Gauze was placed over the site and held between the buttocks. The patient tolerated the procedure well.

Vicryl sutures placed to close the wound?	Yes	No
Specimen sent for histologic evaluation?	Yes	No

Complications: ______________________________

Location of the thromboses: ______________ o'clock on the anal canal with the patient lying in the left lateral decubitus position

Diagnosis: Thrombosed external hemorrhoid—excised

Plan:

- _____ Keep stools soft using stool softeners.
- _____ Limit straining at stool.
- _____ Use stool-bulking agents: Metamucil 1 tablespoon daily in a large glass of orange juice.
- _____ Apply antibiotic ointment to the surgical site daily for 1 week.
- _____ Pain control: three to four tablets ibuprofen with food, or two tablets acetaminophen, every 4 hours if needed.
- _____ Postprocedure instruction sheet given to patient.

Physician: ______________

CC: ______________

CHAPTER 13

Infrared Coagulation of Internal Hemorrhoids

PATIENT INFORMATION

Infrared Coagulation of Internal Hemorrhoids

What are internal hemorrhoids?

All individuals have blood-filled sacs that cushion the anal canal. Chronic trauma and straining during bowel movement can damage the internal tissue support of these sacs, allowing the sacs to swell and further fill with blood. When the sacs enlarge and protrude from the anal canal, they are called hemorrhoids. Internal hemorrhoids form inside the anal canal, whereas external hemorrhoids occur outside the anal canal or on the external skin.

What problems do internal hemorrhoids cause?

Internal hemorrhoids usually are not painful, but they can bleed and itch. Internal hemorrhoids may drip blood into the toilet after a bowel movement, or may produce blood on toilet tissue with wiping. Large internal hemorrhoids protrude through the anal canal and present as a lump that you might be able to feel.

What is infrared coagulation treatment?

Infrared coagulation is a procedure that applies a special type of energy, called infrared, to the base of an internal hemorrhoid. The energy causes scarring within the hemorrhoid, reducing the blood flow in the hemorrhoid and shrinking it. Most people feel a warm or slight burning sensation during the treatment, which lasts only a few minutes. People with extensive hemorrhoids may require more than one treatment.

Are there other treatments for internal hemorrhoids?

Yes. Several other treatments exist for internal hemorrhoids. Older techniques, such as injection of a chemical solution into the hemorrhoid or freezing the hemorrhoid, have been abandoned because of complications. Placing a rubber band at the base of the hemorrhoid causes destruction of the tissue, but can also cause severe infection. Laser surgery can be performed, but is expensive and associated with longer recovery times.

How should I prepare for the procedure?

Take three 200-mg ibuprofen tablets (brand names: Advil, Motrin, Nuprin) with some food about 1 ½ hours before the procedure. About 30 minutes before coming to the office, administer an enema (brand name: Fleet enema) in the rectum. Hold the enema for 5 to 10 minutes, and then expel the fluid and stool. The enema will aid the doctor in performing the procedure.

This handout provides a general overview on this subject and may not apply to everyone. Talk to your family doctor to find out if this information applies to you and to get more information.

PATIENT INSTRUCTIONS

Following Infrared Coagulation of Internal Hemorrhoids

1. You may feel some burning or pain immediately after the procedure. This usually occurs for only a short time. You may take ibuprofen (brand names: Advil, Motrin, Nuprin), four 200-mg tablets three times a day with food, or acetaminophen (brand name: Tylenol), two 325-mg tablets every 6 hours, if needed for discomfort.

2. You should keep your stools soft after any hemorrhoid treatment. You should drink six full glasses of water daily, and take a stool softener (such as Colace or Surfak), two capsules two times a day for at least 2 weeks after the procedure.

3. Many experts recommend long-term treatment with a stool-bulking agent such as Metamucil or Citrucel. Stool-bulking agents can improve the overall health of your colon, and may reduce the risk of colon cancer. Bulking agents can initially produce gas and bloating, but taking stool softeners simultaneously for the first 2 weeks can help until your body adjusts to the stool-bulking agents. Start bulking agents at 1 tablespoon daily and slowly increase.

4. Bloody drainage or mild bleeding with the passage of stools is common in the first few weeks after the procedure. If the bleeding is severe or if you develop a fever, or redness or swelling in the rectal area, please call your doctor. Bleeding often follows passage of hard or watery stools, and these extremes should be avoided.

5. Some people like to take 20-minute sitz baths (soaking in warm tub water) in the first few weeks after the procedure. Sitz baths can aid in healing and reduce discomfort. Over-the-counter preparations, such as Anusol, Tucks pads, or Preparation H, can also be used for symptom control.

6. A proper diet is important for the health of your colon. The National Institutes of Health recommend that you consume five servings of fresh fruits or vegetables daily. The fiber content of fresh vegetables is beneficial to the colon.

7. Straining at stool should be avoided after hemorrhoid treatment. Do not sit for long periods on the toilet, and remove reading materials from the bathroom. Please do not place anything in the rectum, such as an enema, for the first 3 weeks after the procedure.

8. Your doctor may want to examine more of your colon to look for colon disease. This can be done with an examination called flexible sigmoidoscopy, using a flexible lighted tube. The examination is usually performed 6 weeks after the hemorrhoid treatment. Your doctor will give you more information if the procedure is scheduled.

This handout provides a general overview on this subject and may not apply to everyone. Talk to your family doctor to find out if this information applies to you and to get more information.

INFORMED CONSENT FORM

Infrared Coagulation of Internal Hemorrhoids

PATIENT: ______________________________

DATE: ____________________

1. I hereby authorize Dr. ____________________ to perform the procedure known as infrared coagulation of internal hemorrhoids.

2. I understand that this is a procedure performed to eliminate symptomatic internal hemorrhoids. I understand that a small-tipped instrument is placed on the hemorrhoid, and a pulse of infrared energy administered. The energy causes scarring within the hemorrhoid, and reduces blood flow and swelling in the hemorrhoid. I understand that this treatment is administered to an area that usually does not have nerves, but that some discomfort can accompany the procedure. I understand that the practice of medicine is not an exact science, and that no guarantee can be made regarding the outcome of my planned procedure.

3. My doctor has explained to me that this procedure is generally safe, but that certain risks accompany any surgical procedure. Risks associated with infrared coagulation of internal hemorrhoids include:

Bleeding, rarely requiring transfusion or hospitalization

Pain associated with the procedure or the healing process

Excessive scarring and narrowing of the anal canal

Allergic reaction to the numbing medication or surgical instruments

Localized infection in the anal tissues

Rare, unusual reactions, including possible death following any surgical procedure

4. I understand that there are alternatives to the procedure, including surgical removal of the hemorrhoid, laser surgery, electrical burning of the hemorrhoid, or no treatment at all. I understand that these alternate procedures may not offer the same benefits as infrared coagulation. I understand that I can refuse this procedure.

5. I understand that unforeseen conditions may alter the planned procedure. I give permission to my doctor to alter the planned procedure (such as to perform electrosurgery or banding to control excessive bleeding), if necessary, or to administer additional anesthetics or other medication if I should need them for the completion of my procedure.

6. I have read this form and other sheets given to me by my physician. I have had my questions answered to my satisfaction.

WITNESS: ____________________

PATIENT: ____________________

DATE: ____________________

MINOR: ____________________

PARENT: ____________________

NURSING INSTRUCTIONS

Infrared Coagulation of Internal Hemorrhoids

PATIENT PREPARATION

The patient is asked to undress from the waist down, and a drape is placed over the legs and abdomen. The patient can be sitting on the examination table to talk with the physician. The patient will be placed in the left lateral decubitus position, with the left leg extended and the right (upper) leg slightly flexed at the hip and knee. An absorbent pad is placed beneath the patient's buttocks before the start of the procedure.

NONSTERILE PROCEDURE TRAY

Place the following items on a nonsterile drape covering the Mayo stand:

- 2 pairs of nonsterile gloves
- 2 inches of 4 × 4 gauze
- 3 large cotton-tipped swabs
- Ives anoscope
- 1 inch of water-soluble (K-Y) lubricating jelly
- 1 inch of 5% lidocaine ointment

The infrared coagulator is assembled and plugged into the wall outlet, with the timer set at 1.25 seconds

POSTPROCEDURE NURSING INSTRUCTIONS

Wipe away any jelly or drainage from the perianal tissues, if this was not done by the physician at the end of the procedure.

Slowly assist the patient to a standing position, and observe for dizziness or lightheadedness. Encourage the patient to walk; this may help with any discomfort.

Soiled sheets, gauze, or cotton swabs are disposed of in appropriate biohazard waste containers.

Rubbing alcohol on gauze is used to wipe down the outside of the infrared coagulation machine, cord, and application wand.

The tip of the coagulator is unscrewed, washed gently with water and gauze, soaked in glutaraldehyde (Cidex) for 20 minutes, rinsed, and dried before the next use.

PROCEDURE RECORDING FORM

Infrared Coagulation of Internal Hemorrhoids

PATIENT NAME: ____________________

DATE: ____________________

AGE: ____________________

Duration of current hemorrhoid symptoms: ____________________

Circle the Correct Responses:

Anal burning?	Yes	No	Abdominal pain?	Yes	No
Pain with bowel movement?	Yes	No	Anal itching?	Yes	No
Pain between bowel movements?	Yes	No	Prolapse of tissue?	Yes	No
Previous colon cancer?	Yes	No	Fecal incontinence?	Yes	No
Change in stool caliber?	Yes	No	Previous colon polyps?	Yes	No

Previous colon surgery? ____________________
Previous colon examination? ____________________
Medications used for hemorrhoids? ____________________
Previous hemorrhoid surgery? ____________________

IRC Settings:
1.25 seconds ________
1.50 seconds ________
Draw in treatment sites with an "o"

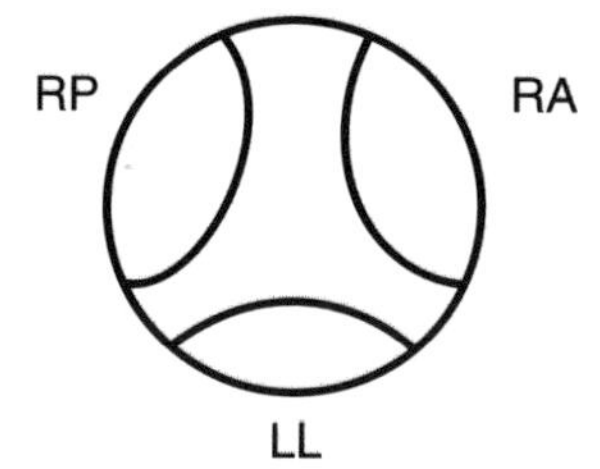

Other findings:
External tags
External hemorrhoids
Anal fissure
Anal fistula

Prostate examination: ____________________

The risks and benefits of the procedure were discussed with the patient, and the patient gave informed consent.
Impression:
Symptomatic internal hemorrhoids grade II and ____________________

Plan:

- ____ Keep stools soft; use stool softeners.
- ____ Eat a high fiber/vegetable/fruit diet
- ____ Drink Metamucil or Citrucel (1 tablespoon in large glass of orange juice daily).
- ____ No reading materials in the bathroom or straining at stool.
- ____ Follow-up in 6 to 12 weeks.
- ____ Flexible sigmoidoscopy discussed, scheduled if desired.
- ____ Postprocedure instruction given to patient.

Physician: ____________________
CC: ____________________

CHAPTER 14

Ingrown Toenail Removal

PATIENT INFORMATION

Ingrown Toenail Removal

What is an ingrown toenail?

An ingrown toenail occurs when the nail edge is damaged and the nail no longer fits properly into the side groove. The nail curls downward and digs into the skin, causing pain, swelling, redness, and drainage. Sometimes a piece of nail (called a lateral pointing spicule) becomes embedded in the side tissue, and the tissue becomes heaped up (hypertrophied).

What causes an ingrown toenail?

There are many causes for ingrown nails, but the two most common causes are poorly-fitting shoes and improperly trimmed nails. Tight shoes compress the side of the nail and alter the fit of the nail in the groove. When nails are peeled off or torn, the edge of the nail can extend down into the corner of the nail groove. A torn nail can irritate the skin next to the nail, producing inflammation (swelling, pain, and redness) and infection.

Can ingrown nails be prevented?

Proper trimming of the nails is the best way to prevent an ingrown nail. Nails should be cut straight across, with the corners of the nail protruding from the end of the toe. Children or teenagers who play with their toes in bed at night can wear socks to bed to keep them from peeling or picking at their toenails.

How can I treat my painful nail?

When an ingrown toenail is mildly inflamed, soaking the foot in warm water and placing dry cotton under the corner of the nail may be all that is needed. If the ingrown toenail worsens, you may develop increasing pain, swelling, and drainage. An antibiotic ointment can be tried at this stage. After you see your doctor for the problem, he or she may try oral antibiotics. Surgical removal of part of the nail is often needed if the problem becomes more severe.

What is the recommended surgical procedure for ingrown nails?

The procedure involves removing a small portion of the lateral side of the nail and destroying the nail bed beneath. The toe is numbed, and the toenail is cut to create a new, straight nail edge. The cells underneath the nail will create a new lateral nail and must be destroyed, thereby creating a permanently thinner nail. If there is heaped up (hypertrophied) tissue on the side of the toe, this also must be destroyed. The toe is then bandaged until it completely heals (a few weeks).

What is the recovery time from my surgery?

You should keep your foot elevated for a few hours and rest the day of the surgery, but then you can return to work or school. You should refrain from running or vigorous exercise for 2 weeks after the surgery.

This handout provides a general overview on this subject and may not apply to everyone. Talk to your family doctor to find out if this information applies to you and to get more information.

PATIENT INSTRUCTIONS

Following Ingrown Toenail Removal

1. Antibiotic ointment will be applied to the toe immediately after the procedure. The ointment is soothing and also promotes faster healing. You should apply the antibiotic ointment twice daily until the wound is completely healed. We like the over-the-counter (nonprescription) antibiotic ointment Mycitracin Plus because of the numbing medication mixed in with the antibiotic.

2. You may shower the day after the surgery. Gently dry the area and apply antibiotic ointment after showering. Avoid bathing, swimming, or soaking the toe for the next 2 weeks. Try to keep the toe clean and dry.

3. Your bandage will help to pad and protect the wound, while absorbing drainage from the wound. You can replace the bandage if blood or fluid soaks the bandage. Please keep the wound bandaged for at least 1 week after the surgery.

4. You may experience some pain after the procedure. If you experience discomfort, you can take ibuprofen (brand names: Advil, Motrin, Nuprin), three 200-mg tablets three times a day with food, and acetaminophen (brand name: Tylenol), two 325-mg tablets every 4 hours.

5. You should wear loose-fitting shoes or sneakers for the first 2 weeks after the procedure. Please avoid wearing high-heeled or tight-fitting shoes in the future. You should avoid running, jumping, or strenuous activity for 2 weeks after the surgery. Teenagers should not participate in physical education for 1 to 2 weeks after the procedure.

6. Infection may develop in the toe in the first few weeks after the surgery. Call your doctor if you develop increasing pain, swelling, redness, or drainage from the toe.

7. Trimming the nails straight across the top of the nail is the best way to prevent another ingrown nail from developing. The nail must not be cut down into the corners, or picked at or torn off. If you should develop another ingrown nail, see your doctor early, as treatment may prevent the need for additional surgery.

This handout provides a general overview on this subject and may not apply to everyone. Talk to your family doctor to find out if this information applies to you and to get more information.

INFORMED CONSENT FORM

Ingrown Toenail Removal

PATIENT: ______________________________

DATE: ____________________

1. I hereby authorize Dr. ____________________ to perform the procedure known as ingrown toenail removal.

2. I understand that this is a procedure performed under local anesthesia to treat the more severe cases of ingrown toenails. The procedure will remove the lateral portion of the nail, creating a straight, new lateral nail edge. Electrosurgery is then used to destroy the cells that form the lateral nail so that a permanently narrowed nail results. This helps to prevent the problem from recurring. Heaped up (hypertrophied) tissue that forms on the side of the toe is also removed. I understand that the practice of medicine is not an exact science, and that no guarantee can be made regarding the outcome of my planned procedure.

3. My doctor has explained to me that this procedure is generally safe, but that certain risks accompany any surgical procedure. Risks associated with ingrown toenail removal include:
   Bleeding, sometimes persisting for days after the procedure
   Pain associated with the surgery or the healing process
   Excessive scarring after the procedure
   Infection in the toe, the bones of the foot, or spreading into the body
   Allergic reaction to the numbing medication or surgical instruments
   Rare, unusual reactions, including possible death from any surgical procedure

4. I understand that there are alternatives to this procedure, including antibiotic therapy, cotton wick insertion below the nail, chemical destruction to the lateral toe, complete removal of the nail, and more extensive laser or surgical procedures. I understand that these alternate procedures may not provide the same benefits as the surgery proposed to me. I understand that I can refuse this procedure.

5. I understand that unforeseen conditions may alter the planned procedure. I give permission to my doctor to alter the planned procedure (such as to suture injured tissue or biopsy unusual growths), if necessary, or to administer additional anesthetics or other medications if I should need them for the completion of my procedure.

6. I have read this form and other sheets given to me by my physician. I have had my questions answered to my satisfaction.

WITNESS: ______________________________

PATIENT: ______________________________

DATE: ______________________________

MINOR: ______________________________

PARENT: ______________________________

NURSING INSTRUCTIONS

Ingrown Toenail Removal

PATIENT PREPARATION

The patient is comfortably seated on the table, with knees bent and feet flat on the table, or legs fully extended and feet extended just beyond the end of the table. An absorbent pad is placed beneath the feet on the table and floor.

NONSTERILE SURGICAL TRAY

A nonsterile drape is placed on a Mayo stand with the following placed on top:

- Nonsterile gloves
- 10-mL syringe filled with 1% lidocaine (Xylocaine), and a 30-gauge needle
- Povidone-iodine solution soaked into 4 × 4 gauze
- 2 inches of 4 × 4 gauze
- Fenestrated drape
- Iris scissors
- Bandage scissors
- 2 pairs of straight hemostats
- Sterile rubber band (if desired)
- Nail splitter (if desired)

ELECTROSURGICAL CART

- Electrosurgical generator
- 2-mm and 4-mm matricectomy electrodes
- 5-mm ball electrode (if desired)
- Smoke evacuator with small particle (viral) filtering system

POSTPROCEDURE DRESSING

- 2 inches of 4 × 4 gauze unfolded into long strips
- Roll of 1-inch tape
- Antibiotic ointment
- Surgical sponge slipper to wear over the bandaged toe

POSTPROCEDURE NURSING INSTRUCTIONS

The antibiotic ointment is liberally applied to the wound. The unfolded gauze is wrapped over the toe, creating a bulky dressing. Longitudinal strips of tape are placed from the top of the foot to the underside of the foot, covering the toe but not constricting blood flow to the toe. The sponge surgical slipper is applied over the entire foot.

Soiled gauze is disposed of in a biohazard waste container. The instruments are washed and sterilized.

The matricectomy electrodes are carefully cleaned of all char, using sandpaper, if needed, on the bare metal portion of the electrode (but not the Teflon-coated side). The electrode should be soaked in disinfectant solution or autoclaved before the next use.

PROCEDURE RECORDING FORM

Ingrown Toenail Removal

PATIENT NAME: ______________________________

AGE: ______________

DATE: ______________

Current symptoms: ______________________________

When symptoms first started: ______________________________

Circle All That Apply:

Trauma Torn nail edge Obesity Diabetes Tight-fitting shoes Subungual mass Onychomycosis

Affected toes:

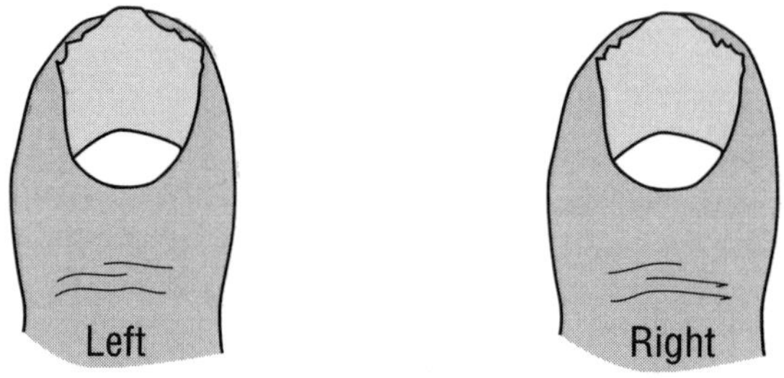

Procedure Description: The toe was prepped with Betadine, and digital block was performed on both sides of the proximal portion of the toe using 1% lidocaine. The patient tolerated the anesthetic well, and good anesthesia was confirmed. A sterile rubber band was placed over the toe, pulled tight, and held in place with a hemostat. The toe was reprepped, draped, and a new lateral nail edge was created by cutting the nail plate from the distal free end of the nail proximally under the proximal nail fold. The lateral piece of nail was then grasped with a hemostat and was removed. The nail bed was dried with gauze, and a 2-mm /4-mm matricectomy electrode was placed over the nail bed and nail matrix. Electrocautery matricectomy was performed with a setting of 4, applied for 2 to 10 seconds, allowing the sparking onto the wound bed. The matrix lateral horn cells were cauterized, and the wound bed was noted to be dry. The lateral nail fold granulation tissue was then cauterized using a ball electrode with a setting of 5, and the ablated tissue was wiped away before additional cautery was applied. The lateral nail fold was treated until a concavity was produced with normal tissue noted at the base. The rubber band was removed, and good hemostasis was noted. Antibiotic ointment was applied, and unfolded gauze was draped over the toe into a bulky dressing. Tape was applied to keep the bandage on overnight, and the patient's foot was placed into a disposable surgical slipper. The postprocedure instructions were given to the patient.
Electrode: 2 mm 4 mm Cutting with: Nail splitter Bandage scissors

Impression: Ingrown toenail

Plan:

____ Keep the foot elevated for a few hours after the procedure.
____ Apply direct pressure to the surgical site if bleeding is noted.
____ Avoid strenuous activity for at least 1 to 2 weeks after the procedure.
____ Apply a topical antibiotic ointment daily (Mycitracin Plus).
____ Call if any signs of infection, redness, pus, swelling, etc.
____ Postprocedure instruction sheet given to patient.

Physician: ______________
CC: ______________

CHAPTER 15

Loop Electrosurgical Excision Procedure

PATIENT INFORMATION

Loop Electrosurgical Excision Procedure (LEEP)

What is the loop electrosurgical excision procedure?

The loop electrosurgical excision procedure (LEEP) is a treatment for cervical disease. LEEP is performed with a thin wire that uses low-voltage electrosurgical energy to remove the diseased tissue. This special wire removes a section of tissue that can be examined under the microscope, but does not injure the tissue remaining on the cervix.

Which women should undergo the LEEP?

LEEP is performed on women with precancerous changes in the cervical tissues. Most women with an abnormal Pap smear initially are evaluated by examination under the microscope with a procedure called colposcopy. If the biopsies performed at colposcopy are significantly abnormal, LEEP can be performed to remove the diseased tissue in an effort to prevent the development of cancer.

Is the procedure safe?

Several studies have demonstrated that LEEP is safe and effective. A coated speculum that does not conduct electric current is used. A coated side wall retractor is used to protect the vaginal walls from any accidental injury. A vacuum is used to remove any smoke that is created during the procedure and to keep anyone from breathing viral particles from the cervix. Your doctor will also make sure that all bleeding from the cervix is stopped at the end of the procedure.

Is LEEP painful?

The cervix is numbed with a local anesthetic for the procedure. About half of patients report that they do not feel the injection of the numbing medicine into the cervix. Take four 200-mg ibuprofen tablets (brand names: Advil, Motrin, Nuprin) before the procedure. The majority of women report that LEEP is very tolerable and more comfortable than colposcopy.

How successful is LEEP?

Studies show that LEEP is more than 95% successful in eliminating precancerous changes of the cervix (dysplasia). The procedure appears to be more successful than older techniques (such as cryosurgery). Women can redevelop dysplasia following LEEP, especially those who continue smoking. It is important to return for scheduled follow-up examinations with your physician after LEEP is performed.

This handout provides a general overview on this subject and may not apply to everyone. Talk to your family doctor to find out if this information applies to you and to get more information.

Following Loop Electrosurgical Excision Procedure (LEEP)

1. You may experience some mild discomfort or cramping following the procedure. You can take ibuprofen (brand names: Advil, Motrin, Nuprin), three 200-mg tablets three times a day, with food to assist with discomfort or cramping. Report severe pain following the procedure to your doctor.

2. Most people feel well immediately following the procedure and can resume normal activities. However, it is recommended that you return home to rest after the procedure.

3. Do not place anything in the vagina for 1 month following the procedure. Tampons should not be used, but sanitary napkins can be used to protect clothing. Avoid sex (intercourse) for 1 month following the procedure.

4. You may experience some bleeding immediately after the procedure, or in 2 to 10 days following the procedure. Most of the late bleeding is associated with ignoring the recommendation to avoid sex (intercourse). Late bleeding can also be associated with straining, riding horseback, or bouncing on a bicycle or in an all-terrain vehicle. Avoid heavy lifting, vigorous physical activity, or straining for the first few weeks following the procedure. If you experience vaginal bleeding for more than 1 week after the procedure, please contact your doctor. If you develop heavy bleeding or are passing clots, please see your doctor.

5. Infection following a LEEP is very uncommon. If you develop severe abdominal pain, fever, or a foul-smelling vaginal discharge, please see your doctor.

6. A brownish iron solution is applied to your cervix at the end of the LEEP to stop bleeding. This solution may cause a brownish-black discharge for 2 weeks following the procedure. Please use sanitary napkins to protect your underwear from the staining that can occur.

7. Please return to have a Pap smear in 4 months. Your doctor will want to examine your cervix with the microscope (colposcope) in 8 months to document the absence of abnormal cells. These follow-up visits are very important to ensure the success of the LEEP.

INFORMED CONSENT FORM

Loop Electrosurgical Excision Procedure (LEEP)

PATIENT: ______________________________

DATE: ____________________

1. I hereby authorize Dr. ____________________ to perform the procedure known as loop electrosurgical excision procedure of the cervix (LEEP).

2. I understand that this is a procedure performed under local anesthesia on the cervix at the base of my uterus (womb). I understand that I have abnormal or precancerous or cancerous cells on my cervix, and that this procedure will attempt to remove all the diseased tissue. I understand that usually this procedure allows me to keep my uterus and to maintain the ability to bear children. I understand that the practice of medicine is not an exact science, and that no guarantee can be made regarding the outcome of my planned procedure.

3. My doctor has explained to me that this procedure is generally safe, but that certain risks accompany any surgical procedure. Risks associated with LEEP of the cervix include:

Bleeding, rarely requiring transfusion or hospitalization

Pain associated with the surgery or the healing process

Localized infection following the procedure

Excessive removal of tissue, resulting in a short and poorly functioning cervix

Narrowing or stenosis of the canal of the cervix

Upward migration of the tissue junction into the canal, making future evaluation of the cervix very difficult

Burns to the tissues outside or inside the vagina

Allergic reaction to the numbing medication or the surgical instruments

Rare, unusual reactions, including possible death following any surgical procedure

4. I understand that there are alternatives to this procedure, including laser procedures, surgical blade procedures, or even removal of the uterus (hysterectomy). I understand that I can refuse this procedure.

5. I understand that unforeseen conditions may alter the planned procedure. I give permission to my doctor to alter the procedure (such as to suture a bleeding vessel), if necessary, or to administer additional anesthetics or other medication if I should need them for the completion of my procedure.

6. I have read this form and other sheets given to me by my physician. I have had my questions answered to my satisfaction.

WITNESS: ______________________

PATIENT: ______________________

DATE: ______________________

MINOR: ______________________

PARENT: ______________________

NURSING INSTRUCTIONS

Loop Electrosurgical Excision Procedure (LEEP)

PREPROCEDURE SETUP

The patient is asked to undress from the waist down, and is draped over the abdomen and legs.

The patient is seated on the examination table to talk with the physician.

The electrosurgical machine, colposcope, and smoke evacuator are plugged in.

The patient can be offered four ibuprofen (Motrin) if not already taken.

Once the patient has spoken with the physician, the patient is placed in the dorsal lithotomy position in stirrups.

The adherent grounding pad is attached to the patient's thigh.

Once the physician inserts the coated speculum, the tubing to the smoke evacuator is attached to the speculum.

NONSTERILE PROCEDURE TRAY

Place the following items on a nonsterile drape covering the Mayo stand:

- Nonsterile gloves and mask
- Ring forceps
- Endocervical curette
- 1/2 inch × 1/2 inch piece of Telfa pad (to remove cervical mucus after the endocervical curettage)
- 1 inch × 1 inch piece of medium sandpaper (for cleaning char from the electrodes)
- Medicine cup with Lugol's (iodine) solution
- Medicine cup with Monsel's paste
- 10-mL syringe filled with 2% lidocaine with epinephrine (Xylocaine with Epinephrine), with a needle extender and a 27-gauge, 1 1/4-inch needle attached
- 12 large cotton-tipped swabs
- 5 small cotton-tipped swabs
- LEEP electrode: 20 mm × 8 mm
- LEEP 5 mm ball electrode
- LEEP electrode for conization: 10 mm × 10 mm
- 3 pathology specimen containers with formalin

POSTPROCEDURE NURSING INSTRUCTIONS

- The electrosurgery machine, colposcope, and smoke evacuator are turned off and unplugged.
- The adherent grounding pad is gently removed from the patient's thigh.
- The patient can be given an adsorbent pad to place inside the underwear.
- The electrode handpiece can be wiped down with a wet towel and then alcohol or glutaraldehyde (Cidex) for subsequent use.
- Soiled or bloody swabs or towels are disposed of in an appropriate biohazard waste container.
- Needles are disposed of in an appropriate sharps container.
- The electrode needles can be cleaned of char using sandpaper, gentle washing, or by activating the electrode inside moist gauze (steam cleaning). The electrodes can be washed in soapy water, and then autoclaved or disinfected in glutaraldehyde.
- The other instruments should be cleaned and autoclaved.

PROCEDURE RECORDING FORM

Loop Electrosurgical Excision Procedure (LEEP)

PATIENT NAME: ______________________________

DATE: ______________

AGE: ______________

Date and result of most recent Pap: ______________
Prior cervical treatment: ______________
Indications for the procedure: ______________

Procedure Description: The patient gave informed consent for the procedure. The patient was placed in the dorsal lithotomy position, and the feet were placed in stirrups. The electrosurgical equipment and smoke evacuator were plugged in and tested. The adhesive return (grounding) pad was placed on the patient's thigh. The nonconducting speculum was inserted into the vagina, and the cervix was visualized. The smoke evacuator tubing was attached to the speculum. The cervix was cleared of mucus and debris, and Lugol's iodine solution was applied to the cervix. Two percent lidocaine with epinephrine was administered intracervically. The patient tolerated the anesthetic well. Additional Lugol's solution was applied. The coated side-wall retractor was applied. An appropriate size loop electrode (20 mm × 8 mm) was selected, and a test pass was performed. There was adequate room for the movement of the electrode. The electrode was activated and passed from 3 to 9 o'clock, including the cervical os in the pass. The tissue was removed with ring forceps and placed in formalin. Additional passes were made to remove any remaining nonstaining ectocervix. Once the entire transformation zone was excised, the 5 mm ball cautery electrode was applied. The outermost edge of the ectocervical excision was cauterized, and any bleeding sites within the wound base were cauterized. If a conization was needed, an additional pass with the 10 mm × 10 mm electrode was performed to remove additional canal tissue. Good hemostasis was achieved, and an endocervical curettage was performed to document a disease-free upper canal. Monsel's paste was applied to the wound base, and the patient tolerated the procedure well. The machines were turned off, and the speculum and instruments were removed.

Complications: ______________________________
Loop electrode selected: 20 mm × 8 mm or other: ______________
Conization performed: ______________________________
Specimens sent: Ectocervix, ECC, and ______________________________
Impressions:

Plan:

- ____ Postoperative instructions reviewed
- ____ Follow-up Pap in 4 months
- ____ Repeat colposcopy in 8 months
- ____ Postprocedure instructions given

Physician: ______________
CC: ______________

CHAPTER 16

No-Scalpel Vasectomy

PATIENT INFORMATION

No-Scalpel Vasectomy

What is a no-scalpel vasectomy?

Vasectomy is a procedure that produces permanent sterilization for men. The no-scalpel procedure is performed by making a single 2-mm puncture in the scrotum and removing a small piece of each vas deferens (the tubes that carry the sperm). By eliminating sperm from the ejaculate (the fluid released during orgasm), pregnancy is prevented. No scalpel is used for cutting in this procedure, and no stitches are needed to close the very small wound.

What happens to the sperm after the surgery?

Sperm continue to be produced in the testicles after the procedure. The sperm continue to be stored in the epididymis (the organ just on top of the testicle). The sperm eventually dissolve and are absorbed by the body. This process of absorption is a natural occurrence (it occurs in men who experience long periods without an ejaculation).

How successful is this surgery?

In general, the procedure is more than 99% effective. Your doctor will ask you to bring semen samples into the office several weeks after your procedure. Your doctor will check for sperm in the samples and notify you of the success of the surgery once two semen specimens are free of sperm. No form of contraception is completely effective, and failures do occur after vasectomy. Until two samples are sperm free, you must use some form of contraception to avoid accidental pregnancy.

Will the vasectomy affect my enjoyment of sex?

No. Erections, climaxes, and ejaculations should continue after vasectomy, just as they were before the procedure. Sometimes removing the fear of an unwanted pregnancy may increase the enjoyment of intercourse. Some men may experience difficulty with erections or ejaculations after the surgery, but this is usually a psychological problem and not a functional complication of the surgery.

What are the complications of the surgery?

In less than 5% of patients, a small blood vessel may continue to bleed, producing a blood clot within the scrotum. However, most blood clots or hematomas resolve on their own. Infection is a rare complication after the operation. A few men develop chronic aching in the scrotum, but this generally lessens over time. A small, tender nodule, called a sperm granuloma, can develop at the cut end of the vas, but this also goes away with time. Some published reports suggest a possible small association between vasectomy and prostate cancer, whereas other reports suggest that there is no connection. Most physicians believe that there is no substantial risk of cancer associated with vasectomy.

Is the surgery reversible?

Vasectomy should not be considered a reversible procedure. Surgery can be performed to reconnect the cut ends of the vas, but there is no guarantee that this surgery can restore fertility. Current techniques for reversal are only about 60% effective. If you have any doubts about permanent sterilization, please consider using temporary birth control measures. Although it is possible to freeze your sperm for future use, having a vasectomy is discouraged unless you are certain you do not want to conceive children in the future.

This handout provides a general overview on this subject and may not apply to everyone. Talk to your family doctor to find out if this information applies to you and to get more information.

PATIENT INSTRUCTIONS

Preparing for No-Scalpel Vasectomy

The following information is provided to help you prepare for the vasectomy procedure.

1. You will need to bring an athletic supporter with you when you come in for the surgery for support and comfort after the procedure. The athletic supporter can be purchased at most pharmacies or retail stores. The supporter will be worn immediately after the procedure.

2. Please avoid aspirin or aspirin-containing medications for 10 days before the procedure. Aspirin can cause you to have bleeding complications from the surgery.

3. The night before the surgery, use scissors to clip the pubic hair on the anterior (at or toward the front) of the scrotum below the base of the penis. Hair on the side of the scrotum and on the lower abdomen wall above the base of the penis does not need to be clipped. Do not shave because shaving increases the chance of infection. Your spouse can assist with the clipping to avoid injuring the skin. Shower after clipping the hairs.

4. Take four 200-mg ibuprofen tablets (brand names: Advil, Motrin, Nuprin) with food 1 hour before coming to the office for the surgery. The ibuprofen will reduce swelling and discomfort associated with the procedure. Ibuprofen should not cause bleeding.

5. You may wish to have someone come with you to the office to drive you home after the procedure. If you chose to take additional medicine, such as Valium, to relax, someone else <u>Must</u> drive you to and from the office because the medicine can make you sleepy. Valium should be taken about a ½ hour before coming to the office. If you want to take this medicine, ask your doctor for a prescription.

6. Please feel free to ask any additional questions you may have.

PATIENT INSTRUCTIONS

Following No-Scalpel Vasectomy

1. Antibiotic ointment, gauze, and an athletic supporter will be placed over the wound immediately after the procedure. Continue to apply the antibiotic ointment daily until the skin puncture site is completely healed. Wear the athletic supporter for at least 24 hours.

2. Once you return home after the surgery, elevate your feet and place an ice bag over the scrotal area to reduce swelling. Take it easy for the rest of the day. You can spend more time walking on the second day. Do not shower for 24 hours after surgery. Heavy lifting or vigorous physical activity should be avoided for 1 to 2 weeks.

3. Patients often notice scrotal swelling in the first week after the surgery. The swelling often increases with activity and may be relieved by wearing an athletic supporter and resting.

4. If you experience pain or discomfort, you may take a combination of ibuprofen (brand names: Advil, Motrin, Nuprin), three or four 200-mg tablets three times a day with food, and acetaminophen (brand name: Tylenol), two 325-mg tablets every 4 hours. If you experience increasing pain, please call your doctor.

5. Infection is very uncommon after the no-scalpel vasectomy procedure. Call your doctor if you notice excessive redness, tenderness, warmth, or drainage from the surgical site.

6. Bruising over the scrotal skin is common after vasectomy. However, if the scrotal sac is bruised and expanding in size, please call your doctor.

7. Some men develop a small, tender nodule where the vas deferens was cut (called sperm granulomas). These can produce discomfort, but almost always go away on their own. You can ask your doctor to reexamine the site if you are concerned.

8. You may have sexual intercourse 1 week after the surgery. The first time you have sex you may notice some discomfort from the cut tubes. During the second week, you may have sex two or three times. The third week you can resume your normal routine. However, another form of contraception (such as condoms) should be used until you have been told that you have had two sperm-free semen samples.

9. Two separate semen evaluations must be performed to document the success of the vasectomy. The first specimen is examined in 6 to 10 weeks, or after about 20 ejaculations. The second specimen is examined 6 weeks after the first sample, or after about 40 ejaculations. Bring the specimens to the office in the container given to you at the time of the surgery. The specimens should be brought to the office within 1 to 2 hours of the ejaculation. There is no charge for the first two specimens. Although it is usually not necessary, semen can be checked again some years after the surgery if you desire continued reassurance that the vasectomy was successful.

This handout provides a general overview on this subject and may not apply to everyone. Talk to your family doctor to find out if this information applies to you and to get more information.

VASECTOMY COUNSELING FORM

No-Scalpel Vasectomy

To Be Completed by the Patient:

NAME: ______________________ DATE: ____________

AGE: ________ OCCUPATION: ______________________

IF MARRIED, WIFE'S NAME: ______________________

WIFE'S AGE: ________

CHILDREN'S NAME(s), AGE(s): ______________________

Circle the Correct Responses:

Is your current relationship with your wife or partner stable?	Yes	No
Do you have any problems with sexual functioning?	Yes	No
Do you have a religious conflict with vasectomy?	Yes	No
Are you sure you want to undergo a permanent sterilization procedure?	Yes	No
If your youngest child were lost to illness, would that change your desire for permanent sterilization?	Yes	No
Do you want to take Valium for additional relaxation before the procedure?	Yes	No

Past Medical History:

History of hernia surgery?	Yes	No
Prior psychological counseling?	Yes	No
Prior mumps in the testicle?	Yes	No
Do you take aspirin?	Yes	No
Any prior major illnesses?	Yes	No
History of bleeding disorders?	Yes	No

Medication Allergies: ______________________

Routine medications taken: ______________________

To Be Completed by the Physician:

Physical Examination:

Hernias?	Yes	No
Vas palpated bilaterally?	Yes	No
Testicles palpate normally?	Yes	No
Varicocele absent bilaterally?	Yes	No
Urethral discharge?	Yes	No
Scrotal skin normal?	Yes	No
Valium prescription given?	Yes	No
Preprocedure videotape viewed?	Yes	No

Impression and Plan: The patient desires permanent sterilization. The patient is aware of the risks and benefits of the surgery. The information packet and counseling diagram were given to the patient. The patient has been counseled about the possible association between vasectomy and prostate cancer. The patient has been scheduled for the procedure; informed consent has been signed and is included in the chart.

Physician: ______________

CC: ______________

Date of surgery: ______________

Postprocedure evaluation:

Result:

		Date	Nurse initials	Patient initials
Semen check #1:	NSS	______	______	______
Semen check #2:	NSS	______	______	______

(Circle NSS if no sperm are seen)

COUNSELING CHECKLIST

No-Scalpel Vasectomy

PATIENT: ______________________ **DATE:** __________

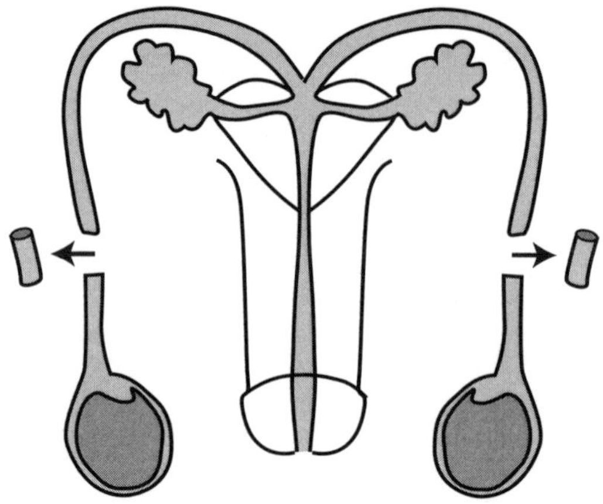

1. Procedure Description

____ Local anesthesia is used for the procedure.
____ A small puncture is performed that does not require suture closure.
____ A 1/4-inch to 1/2-inch portion of the vas is removed and saved until the semen checks are clear.
____ The cut ends of the vas are sealed with a battery heat cautery unit.
____ A small metal clip is used on the fascial tissue to separate the cut ends of the vas.

2. Procedure Effects

____ About the same amount of ejaculate is produced, even without the sperm present.
____ Problems with ejaculates/erections are probably psychological.
____ Postoperative pain or aching possible.
____ Bleeding/infections/sperm granulomas are uncommon.
____ Sterilization procedures are not 100% successful.
____ Possible association with prostate cancer.

3. Preparing for the Procedure

____ Clip the hair on the anterior scrotum the night before the procedure.
____ Take four ibuprofen about 1 hour before the procedure.
____ Bring an athletic supporter when presenting for the surgery.

4. Postoperative Instructions

____ Wear the athletic supporter for 1 to 2 days.
____ Most men return to work in 3 days.
____ Attempt sexual intercourse in 1 week, twice during the second week, and then as desired.
____ Blood or pain may accompany the first ejaculation.
____ First semen check after 20 ejaculations (usually 6 to 12 weeks), then second check about 6 weeks later.

Physician: ______________________
CC: ______________________

INFORMED CONSENT FORM

No-Scalpel Vasectomy

PATIENT: ____________________

DATE: ____________________

1. I hereby authorize Dr. ____________________ to perform the procedure known as the no-scalpel vasectomy procedure.

2. I understand that the no-scalpel vasectomy procedure is a surgical technique for permanent sterilization. After this procedure I should be unable to impregnate a woman. It has been explained to me that no form of sterilization, including vasectomy, is completely effective in preventing pregnancy. I understand that the procedure will remove a small portion of my vas deferens (the tubes that carry the sperm). A small metal clip will be used to seal a layer of tissue between the cut ends of the vas, thereby reducing the chance of a procedure failure. I understand that the practice of medicine is not an exact science, and that no guarantee can be made regarding the outcome of my planned procedure.

3. My doctor has explained to me that this procedure is generally safe, but that risks accompany any surgical procedure. Risks associated with the no-scalpel vasectomy procedure include:
   - Bleeding, occasionally requiring drainage from the scrotum
   - Pain from the procedure or chronic aching after the procedure
   - Excessive scarring, especially if the tissue does not heal normally
   - Allergic reaction to the numbing medication or the surgical instruments
   - Infection in the tissues after the procedure
   - Potential for long-term effects including possible prostate cancer
   - Failure of the procedure to produce permanent sterilization
   - Rare, unusual reactions, including possible death following any surgical procedure

4. I understand that there are alternatives to this procedure, including nonpermanent contraceptive choices, or permanent female sterilization. I have been advised not to undergo this procedure if there is a chance that I might want to have (more) children in the future. I understand that I can refuse this surgery.

5. I understand that unforeseen conditions may alter the planned procedure. I give permission to my doctor to alter the procedure (such as to make incisions in the scrotum if the no-scalpel technique cannot be performed), if necessary, or to administer additional anesthetics or other medication if I should need them for the completion of my procedure.

6. I have read this form and others given to me by my physician. I have had my questions answered to my satisfaction.

WITNESS: ____________________

PATIENT: ____________________

DATE: ____________________

SPOUSE OR PARTNER: ____________________

NURSING INSTRUCTIONS

No-Scalpel Vasectomy

PATIENT PREPARATION

The procedure trays are prepared before the patient is brought to the procedure room. The patient is asked to undress from the waist down, including removal of the underwear. The patient is given a disposable sheet, and asked to sit on the table once undressed. At the start of the procedure the patient is lies supine, with the legs extended and separated. An absorbable pad is placed beneath the patient. Obtain the athletic supporter from the patient and place it on the nonsterile tray. In general, the nurse is not in the room during the procedure.

NONSTERILE TRAY FOR ANESTHESIA/POSTOPERATIVE CARE

Place the following items on a nonsterile sheet covering the Mayo stand:

- Nonsterile gloves
- Povidone-iodine solution soaked into a 4 × 4 gauze (in a sterile basin)
- 10-mL syringe filled with 1% lidocaine (Xylocaine), and a 25-gauge 1 1/4-inch needle
- Antibiotic ointment
- 2 inches of nonsterile 4 × 4 gauze
- Patient-supplied athletic supporter
- 2 postoperative semen collection containers (in a plastic bag)
- Formalin container for the excised portions of vas deferens
- Basin with sterile saline poured onto 1 inch of 4 × 4 gauze

STERILE TRAY FOR THE PROCEDURE

Place the following items on a sterile sheet covering the Mayo stand:

- Sterile gloves
- Sterile fenestrated drape
- Sterile nonfenestrated drape
- Vas dissecting forceps
- Atraumatic vas clamp
- Disposable battery cautery unit placed inside of a sterile glove
- 2 inches of sterile 4 × 4 gauze
- 2 pair of straight hemostats
- 1 curved hemostat and 1 pair of Iris scissors
- Surgical clip (Hemoclip) applicator
- 1 container (clip) of medium metal surgical clips (Hemoclip)

POSTPROCEDURE NURSING INSTRUCTIONS

The patient is given the postoperative semen specimen containers and the specimens of the vas deferens in formalin.

Disposable needles are disposed of in an appropriate sharps container.

Bloody gauze is disposed of in an appropriate biohazard container.

The instruments are scrubbed, washed, rinsed, and dried. Place the instruments in a clear sterilization packet, either individually or as a surgical tray, and sterilize in the autoclave.

The battery cautery unit cannot be submersed. Remove the tip (if removable). The tip can be cleaned by scraping off char, rinsed with water, and then activated on the battery unit for 15 seconds. The tip should be soaked in glutaraldehyde for at least 20 minutes, rinsed, and dried before the next use. The tip should be activated and cooled immediately before being placed inside the sterile glove for the next procedure.

PROCEDURE RECORDING FORM

No-Scalpel Vasectomy

PATIENT NAME: ____________________

DATE: ____________________

Procedure Description: The patient was previously counseled and gave informed consent for the procedure. Any remaining patient questions were answered before the procedure. The patient lay supine on the table. The penis, scrotum, and upper inner thigh were washed with a povidone-iodine solution, and the penis was lifted cephalad. The right vas was swung to the midline using the three-finger technique. The skin of the anterior scrotum over the median raphe was anesthetized using 1% lidocaine. The 25-gauge 1 1/4-inch needle was then inserted alongside the right vas in the upper scrotum and an external spermatic sheath block was accomplished. The needle was withdrawn. The left vas was swung to the middle, and the left side was anesthetized in the same fashion as the right. The patient tolerated the anesthesia well.

Sterile gloves were applied, the scrotum was reprepped with povidone-iodine solution, and sterile drapes were placed. The right vas was swung to the midline using the three-finger technique. The right vas was grasped just below the anesthetized skin using the vas clamp. The skin above the vas was punctured using the vas dissecting forceps. The skin was spread, and the vas forceps were used to lift the vas through the puncture site. The loop of vas was regrasped using the vas clamp. The fascial tissues were dissected off the vas. The vas was hemitransected on both sides of the loop of elevated vas. The proximal and distal ends of the tube (that will remain within the scrotum) were sealed using the battery cautery unit. The proximal (testicular) vas was then fully transected, and the cut end of the tube retracted back into the scrotum. The fascial tissues were elevated and sealed over this end of the tube using a medium metal Hemoclip. The distal (abdominal) end of the vas was fully transected, and a 1/4- to 1/2-inch piece of vas (top of the loop) placed in formalin. The cut distal end of the vas protruded above the metal clip on the fascia, and the proximal cut end was below. Good hemostasis was noted, and the right side was returned to the scrotum. The left vas was swung to the midline, and grasped through the puncture site using the vas clamp. The left vas was delivered through the skin, and the same procedure that was performed on the right was performed on the left side.

The patient tolerated the procedure well. The scrotum was washed off using saline or water. Good hemostasis was noted at the skin puncture site. Antibiotic ointment and gauze were placed over the site beneath the athletic supporter. The patient was given postoperative instructions, and was instructed to return if problems develop. The need for additional contraception until the two postoperative semen checks are clear was emphasized to the patient. The patient will return for postoperative semen checks in 6 and 12 weeks. The vas specimens were given to the patient to keep in a safe location until the semen checks are completed. Two specimen containers were given to the patient.

Premedication for the procedure:
Four 200-mg ibuprofen _____
Two 5-mg Valium _____
Difficulty in isolating the vas? Yes No Side: ____________________

Complications: ____________________
Changes to the procedure or other findings:

Other instructions:

Physician: ____________________
CC: ____________________

CHAPTER 17

Skin Cryosurgery

PATIENT INFORMATION

Skin Cryosurgery

What is skin cryosurgery?

Skin cryosurgery is a simple, efficient, and effective treatment used to remove a wide variety of skin lesions or growths. The process uses a controlled amount of freezing to the skin, resulting in the death of the unwanted skin growth. The treatment can be performed with a small probe or with the direct application of a freezing solution to the skin.

What are the advantages of skin cryosurgery?

Cryosurgery is an easy technique for both the doctor and the patient. There is usually little scarring after this treatment, and the procedure is bloodless and does not require sutures (stitches). Most people feel little discomfort from the procedure, because the technique tends to numb the skin. This technique usually requires fewer office visits for follow-up than other surgical removal procedures. Infection rates may be lower with this technique.

What are some of the skin growths that can be treated with cryosurgery?

Most types of warts can be effectively treated by cryosurgery. Precancerous, sun-damaged skin areas (actinic keratoses) are also commonly treated with this technique. Many benign (noncancerous) skin growths, such as pyogenic granulomas and dermatofibromas, also respond well to this procedure. Cryosurgery can be performed to treat certain skin cancers.

What complications can develop after this procedure?

Cryosurgery can cause permanent lightening of the skin. Nerves below the treated area can be damaged, resulting in short-term or permanent numbness. Skin with reduced blood supply can develop a sore (ulcer) or an exaggerated response to the treatment. However, excessive scarring or infection are uncommon after cryosurgery.

Will I feel pain during or after the procedure?

Most people feel a burning sensation during the procedure. The burning sensation may become stronger as the frozen skin begins to thaw. Many people describe it as the feeling of an ice cube stuck to the skin. Most adults find the discomfort quite tolerable; young children may cry during the procedure.

This handout provides a general overview on this subject and may not apply to everyone. Talk to your family doctor to find out if this information applies to you and to get more information.

PATIENT INSTRUCTIONS

Following Skin Cryosurgery

1. After cryosurgery, the skin site often develops a blister, turns black, or forms a scab. Over the next few weeks, the dead skin (and unwanted skin growth) will fall off. Please do not pick at the site or pull the scab off, because it will interfere with the healing process.

2. If a large, painful blister develops at the treatment site, the blister can be drained to provide some relief. It is recommended that you return to the office to have the doctor drain the blister, unless instructed otherwise. Most blisters eventually drain on their own.

3. Burning and stinging may occur at the treatment site for several hours after cryosurgery. If you experience discomfort, you can take ibuprofen (brand names: Advil, Motrin, Nuprin), three 200-mg tablets three times a day with food, or acetaminophen (brand name: Tylenol), two 325-mg tablets every 4 hours.

4. You may shower, get the site wet, and resume normal activities immediately after cryosurgery. You don't have to cover the treatment site with a Band-Aid after the first day. Antibiotic ointment can be applied to the wound each day, if desired, and a Band-Aid used to reduce rubbing at the site.

5. Infection is very uncommon after cryosurgery. If you develop increasing redness, tenderness, or drainage, please call your doctor.

6. Once the growth comes off, the skin beneath the site usually appears red. Over several months, the area will gradually appear the color of normal skin. The area can be itchy or sensitive to touch at first, but this goes away over time.

7. Nerve injury can occur when freezing is performed close to skin nerves. If you develop numbness after cryosurgery, it often goes away in 6 weeks. If problems persist, see your doctor.

8. A second cryosurgical session may be required to treat a skin growth. Please follow-up in 1 month, or as instructed by your doctor, so the treatment site can be reexamined.

INFORMED CONSENT FORM

Skin Cryosurgery

PATIENT: ______________________________

DATE: ____________________

1. I hereby authorize Dr. ____________________ to perform the procedure known as skin cryosurgery.

2. I understand that this is a procedure performed to destroy abnormal skin growths and tumors. I understand that the procedure can be used on benign, precancerous, or cancerous growths. Cryosurgery uses a special tip that freezes the growth, and then the area blisters and falls off. It is hoped that this procedure will remove the lesion and prevent recurrence. I understand that the practice of medicine is not an exact science, and that no guarantee can be made regarding the outcome of my planned procedure.

3. My doctor has explained to me that this procedure is generally safe, but that certain risks can accompany any surgical procedure. Risks associated with skin cryosurgery include:

   Bleeding, bruising, excessive blistering or infection at the treatment site

   Pain associated with the treatment or the healing process

   Excessive scarring or permanent skin lightening at the treatment site

   Allergic reaction to the numbing medication or the materials and chemicals used in the procedure

   Excessive reaction to the freezing, producing skin breakdown

   Damage to the structures beneath the skin including arteries and nerves

   Rare, unusual reactions, including possible death following any surgical procedure

4. I understand that there are alternatives to this procedure, including surgical removal of the growth, chemical or laser destruction of the growth, or no treatment at all. I understand that I can refuse this procedure.

5. I understand that unforeseen conditions may alter the planned procedure. I give permission to my doctor to alter the procedure (such as to remove fluid from a rapidly forming blister), if necessary, or to administer additional anesthetics or other medications if I should need them for the completion of my procedure.

6. I have read this form and other sheets given to me by my physician. I have had my questions answered to my satisfaction.

WITNESS: ______________________

PATIENT: ______________________

DATE: ______________________

MINOR: ______________________

PARENT: ______________________

NURSING INSTRUCTIONS

Skin Cryosurgery

PREPROCEDURE NURSING INSTRUCTIONS

The patient is seated comfortably on the examination table, and the areas to be treated are exposed for the physician.

The cryosurgical tank, attached pressure gauge, and cryosurgical administration unit are inspected. The attachments are checked, and the absence of leakage confirmed. The valve to the cryosurgical tank is opened, and the tank pressure is noted to be adequate (in the green). The tank should be replaced if inadequate pressure is noted (in the yellow or red).

NONSTERILE TRAY USED FOR THE PROCEDURE

Place the following items on a nonsterile drape covering the Mayo stand:

- Nonsterile gloves
- 1 inch of 4 × 4 gauze
- 1 inch of water-soluble jelly (K-Y jelly)
- Dermal tips for the cryosurgery unit
- Antibiotic ointment
- Bandage

POSTPROCEDURE NURSING INSTRUCTIONS

The jelly is wiped off the patient, and the antibiotic ointment and bandage are applied to the treatment site.

The dermal tips used for the procedure are washed in soap and water, and then soaked in glutaraldehyde (Cidex) for at least 20 minutes before being rinsed with water, dried, and used again.

Any soiled or bloody gauze is disposed of in an appropriate biohazard waste container.

The postprocedure instruction sheet is given to the patient.

PROCEDURE RECORDING FORM

Skin Cryosurgery

PATIENT NAME: ______________________________

AGE: ______________

DATE: ______________

Have you had in the past or do you now have any of the following?

Cancer?	Yes	No	Macroglobulinemia?	Yes	No
Multiple myeloma?	Yes	No	Lymphoma?	Yes	No
Systemic lupus erythematosus?	Yes	No	Rheumatoid arthritis?	Yes	No
Syphilis?	Yes	No	Polyarteritis nodosum?	Yes	No
Ulcerative colitis?	Yes	No	Cytomegalovirus infection?	Yes	No
Hepatitis B infection?	Yes	No	Cryoglobulinemia?	Yes	No
Poststreptococcal glomerulonephritis?	Yes	No	High-dose steroid therapy?	Yes	No
Epstein-Barr virus infection?	Yes	No			

Lesion 1

Location: ______________________________
Symptoms: ______________________________
Clinical impression: ______________________________

Lesion 2

Location: ______________________________
Symptoms: ______________________________
Clinical impression: ______________________________

Lesion 3

Location: ______________________________
Symptoms: ______________________________
Clinical impression: ______________________________

Lesion 4

Location: ______________________________
Symptoms: ______________________________
Clinical impression: ______________________________

Procedure Description: The skin was cleansed of dirt and debris. Hyperkeratotic lesions were pared down with a No. 15 blade. The proper-sized cryosurgical tip was selected. The tip was attached to the cryogun, and a water-soluble gel was applied to the tip. The tip was positioned over the lesion, the cryogun was activated, and the freeze duration was determined by the extension of the ice ball to 2 to 5 mm beyond the edge of the lesion. The lesion was thawed, and a repeat freeze was applied. Antibiotic ointment and a bandage were applied to the site.

Anesthesia administered: ______________________________
Complications: ______________________________

Impression: Cryosurgical destruction of skin lesions, number ______________

Plan:

- ____ Keep site clean and dry.
- ____ Follow up if excessive blistering, pain, skin breakdown.
- ____ Postprocedure instruction sheet was given to the patient.

Physician: ______________
CC: ______________

SECTION III

DIAGNOSTIC AND THERAPEUTIC PROCEDURES

CHAPTER 18

Dermal Electrosurgery Shave Excision

PATIENT INFORMATION

Dermal Electrosurgery Shave Excision

What is dermal electrosurgery shave excision?

Dermal electrosurgery shave excision is a procedure used to remove skin tumors or other skin growths. The technique involves shaving the lesion off the skin, without penetrating beneath the skin. Electrosurgery is used to remove any remaining tumor cells from the base of the wound, while smoothing the wound edges. Electrosurgery attempts to improve the final scar appearance without damaging the healthy tissues below the surgery site.

What are the benefits of a shave excision?

Shave excision is a simpler and less expensive procedure than a full-thickness skin excision that requires sutures (stitches). Shave excisions do not need sutures or a return visit for suture removal. All surgical skin procedures produce a scar, but the shave excision with electrosurgical smoothing of the wound edges can produce a less noticeable scar that blends well into the surrounding skin. Infections are infrequent after shave procedures, and the shave procedure provides a specimen for analysis.

What type of anesthesia is used for this procedure?

Most shave excisions are performed with local anesthesia. The numbing medicine is injected beneath the skin growth using a very small needle, and the lesion is raised upward by the anesthetic fluid. The numbing medicine actually makes the shave procedure easier to perform.

What happens to the skin growth once it is removed?

Once a skin tumor or skin growth is removed, it is sent to the hospital where it is examined under the microscope by a specialist physician known as a pathologist. The pathologic evaluation can determine whether the skin growth is cancerous.

Will the scar go away after this procedure?

All skin surgeries produce some scarring. At first, the scar will be red. You shouldn't worry, though, because most scars will eventually lighten over the next year. Avoid getting the wound sunburned for several months after the surgery to prevent the scar from getting darker.

This handout provides a general overview on this subject and may not apply to everyone. Talk to your family doctor to find out if this information applies to you and to get more information.

PATIENT INSTRUCTIONS

Following Dermal Electrosurgery Shave Excision

1. Your doctor has applied a solution to stop bleeding from the wound base. The solution may make the wound appear dark or brown, but the color should fade as the wound heals.

2. After washing the surgical site, the nurse will apply antibiotic ointment to cover the wound. The ointment is soothing and promotes faster healing. You should apply antibiotic ointment twice daily until the wound is completely healed. The over-the-counter (nonprescription) antibiotic ointment Mycitracin Plus has numbing medicine added to the antibiotic.

3. You will have a Band-Aid applied to cover the wound. The bandage protects the wound from rubbing against clothing, and absorbs any drainage that may occur. You can remove the bandage at any time. You should reapply a Band-Aid to the site whenever you are in sunlight (for several months after the procedure) to prevent a sunburn to the site. Sunburn can lead to darkening of the wound.

4. Some people experience a burning sensation at the wound site. If you experience discomfort, you can take acetaminophen (brand name Tylenol), two 325-mg tablets every 4 hours, or ibuprofen (brand names: Advil, Motrin, Nuprin), three 200-mg tablets three times a day with food, for the first few days after the surgery.

5. Infection rarely follows the electrosurgery shave excision. If your wound develops signs of infection such as pus, marked tenderness, swelling, or increasing redness, please call your doctor.

6. Skin tumors can sometimes grow back. If your skin growth was removed and then appears to come back, please return to your doctor for a follow-up exam.

7. Excessive scarring sometimes follows a shave excision procedure. If you notice that the scar is growing, becomes hard or nodular, or raised and dome-shaped, please see your doctor.

8. Most shave excision scars appear red during the first few weeks after the procedure, and may be unsightly. Be patient with your scar; scars that appear unsightly at the start often become very acceptable over the next year's time.

This handout provides a general overview on this subject and may not apply to everyone. Talk to your family doctor to find out if this information applies to you and to get more information.

INFORMED CONSENT FORM

Dermal Electrosurgery Shave Excision

PATIENT: ______________________________

DATE: ____________________

1. I hereby authorize Dr. ____________________ to perform the procedure known as the dermal electrosurgery shave excision.

2. I understand that this is a procedure performed under local anesthesia to remove skin growths or tumors. I understand that the physician will attempt to remove the entire lesion to prevent regrowth, while also trying to optimize the final cosmetic result. I understand that this procedure usually yields acceptable scars, but that each person heals differently. I understand that the practice of medicine is not an exact science, and that no guarantee can be made regarding the outcome of my planned procedure.

3. My doctor has explained to me that this procedure is generally safe but that certain risks accompany any surgical procedure. Risks associated with the dermal electrosurgery shave excision procedure include:

Bleeding from the surgical site

Unintentional burn to skin (either nearby or distant)

Damage to structures or tissues beneath the treatment site

Excessive scarring from the procedure

Allergic reaction to the medications or surgical instruments

Infection in the tissues after the procedure

Rare, unusual reactions, including possible death following any surgical procedure

4. I understand that there are alternatives to this procedure, including full-thickness skin excision, laser destruction, freezing or cryotherapy, or chemical destruction of the growth. I understand that the alternate procedures may not yield the same benefits as the shave excision procedure. I understand that I can refuse this procedure.

5. I understand that unforeseen conditions may alter the planned procedure. I give permission to my doctor to alter the procedure (such as to excise the area with a standard excision), if necessary, or to administer additional anesthetics or other medications if I should need them for the completion of my procedure.

6. I have read this form and other sheets given to me by my physician. I have had my questions answered to my satisfaction.

WITNESS: ______________________

PATIENT: ______________________

DATE: ______________________

MINOR: ______________________

PARENT: ______________________

NURSING INSTRUCTIONS

Dermal Electrosurgery Shave Excision

PATIENT PREPARATION

The patient is seated or lying comfortably. An absorbent sheet is placed beneath the site to be treated in the event any blood or fluid drains away from the treatment site (e.g., under the arm or over the collar around the neck). The electrosurgery return (antennae) plate is placed beneath the patient (it only needs to be near the patient to collect stray current).

NONSTERILE TRAY FOR THE PROCEDURE

A nonsterile drape is placed on a Mayo stand with the following on top:

- Nonsterile gloves
- 1 inch of nonsterile 4 × 4 gauze
- A 5- or 10-mL syringe is filled with 2% lidocaine (Xylocaine) (with or without epinephrine) with a 30-gauge needle attached
- Povidone-iodine solution on 4 × 4 gauze
- No. 15 scalpel blade
- 12 small cotton-tipped applicators
- A small disposable plastic (medicine) cup containing Monsel's solution
- A small disposable plastic (medicine) cup containing 80% aluminum chloride (if lesion removed is on the face)
- Formalin container

EQUIPMENT ON THE ELECTROSURGICAL CART

Electrosurgical generator

Smoke evacuator with a special small particle (viral) filtration system

Small dermal loop electrodes

PROCEDURE NURSING INSTRUCTIONS

Hold the end of the vacuum tubing near the surgical site and activate the smoke evacuator during electrosurgery. For hemostasis, hand the cotton-tipped applicators with Monsel's solution (or aluminum chloride) to the physician (to prevent extensive reaching over the patient).

POSTPROCEDURE NURSING INSTRUCTIONS

1. Cleanse the wound with water or saline on gauze. Apply antibiotic ointment and bandage to the surgical site.

2. Dispose of soiled gauze in a biohazard waste container. Dispose of the blade and needle in a sharps container.

3. The electrodes are cleansed of char, washed and soaked in glutaraldehyde (Cidex), or autoclaved before the next use.

PROCEDURE RECORDING FORM

Dermal Electrosurgery Shave Excision

PATIENT NAME: ____________________

AGE: ____________

DATE: ____________

Lesion 1

Location: ____________________
Symptoms: ____________________
Clinical impression: ____________________

Sent for histology?	Yes	No	Irritation from clothing or jewelry?	Yes	No
Bleeding?	Yes	No	Pain or tenderness?	Yes	No
Inflamed?	Yes	No			

Lesion 2

Location: ____________________
Symptoms: ____________________
Clinical impression: ____________________

Sent for histology?	Yes	No	Irritation from clothing or jewelry?	Yes	No
Bleeding?	Yes	No	Pain or tenderness?	Yes	No
Inflamed?	Yes	No			

Lesion 3

Location: ____________________
Symptoms: ____________________
Clinical impression: ____________________

Sent for histology?	Yes	No	Irritation from clothing or jewelry?	Yes	No
Bleeding?	Yes	No	Pain or tenderness?	Yes	No
Inflamed?	Yes	No			

Other lesions: ____________________

Procedure Description: The patient gave informed consent for the procedure. Other options were discussed, and the patient elected to undergo electrosurgical shave excision. The lesion and surrounding skin were prepped with povidone-iodine solution and anesthetized using 2% lidocaine (with epinephrine). The patient tolerated the anesthesia well. Sharp excision was carried out using a No. 15 blade held horizontal to the skin surface. Monsel's solution was applied with a cotton-tipped applicator to the wound base for hemostasis. Electrosurgical feathering was carried out using a cutting current and a setting of 1.5 to 3.0 (15 to 30 W). The wound edges were gently blended into the surrounding skin to improve the final scar result. Monsel's solution again was applied for hemostasis, and antibiotic ointment and a bandage was placed over the wound.

Complications: ____________________

Plan:

____ Patient will be notified of the histology results.
____ Patient was asked to be patient as the scar matures over time.
____ Patient will return if excessive scar or lesion recurrence are noted.
____ Patient was informed to return if the lesion appears infected.
____ Postprocedure instructions were given to the patient.

Physician: ____________________
CC: ____________________

CHAPTER 19

Fine-Needle Aspiration of the Breast

PATIENT INFORMATION

Fine-Needle Aspiration of the Breast

What is fine-needle aspiration?

Fine-needle aspiration is a simple, cost-effective technique to diagnose many benign and malignant breast diseases. During this procedure, a thin needle is placed within a breast lump. If the lump is a simple cyst, the fluid within the cyst is removed into a syringe. If the lump is a solid growth, then the tip of the needle is passed back and forth multiple times within the growth to obtain cells for further analysis.

Is fine-needle aspiration uncomfortable?

Most women report that the discomfort is very minor. The skin over the breast lump can be numbed. However, many women believe that the anesthetic (numbing medicine) burns as much as the needle insertion and aspiration, and they choose not to receive the anesthetic.

What are the possible benefits of undergoing this procedure?

In the past, many women routinely underwent surgery to find out the nature of their breast lump. Needle aspiration can help to reduce the need for more extensive surgical procedures. If the lump is a cyst, draining it can reduce discomfort and may make it go away. If the lump is solid, the cells within the lump can be sent to the hospital for examination under the microscope to check for malignancy (cancer) in the lump.

How accurate is needle aspiration?

Fine-needle aspiration is not a perfect test, and it is possible that this technique may not detect a cancer. However, it is usually done in combination with a physical exam and a mammogram. Therefore, a normal report is very reassuring when the mammogram and physical exam are also normal. If any one of the tests is not normal, a surgical biopsy may be needed.

Are there any risks to this procedure?

The risks of needle aspiration are relatively minor. Bruising can develop in the breast tissue after the needle insertion. Discomfort usually is mild and doesn't last long. Very rarely, the needle can introduce air around the lung if it is inserted too deeply beneath the breast. Infection has been rarely reported after this procedure.

If the report on the cells in my breast is normal, do I need any further follow-up?

Despite a reassuring report, it is very important that you follow-up with your doctor as directed. You may be asked to have another physical exam or mammogram within the next year.

This handout provides a general overview on this subject and may not apply to everyone. Talk to your family doctor to find out if this information applies to you and to get more information.

PATIENT INSTRUCTIONS

Following Fine-Needle Aspiration of the Breast

1. Your doctor will ask you to hold direct pressure on the aspiration site for 5 to 10 minutes after the procedure. You will be given some gauze to put over the site when you apply this pressure. Despite this, you may still develop bruising in the breast after the procedure. If you notice extensive bruising, or if the breast is enlarging in size from swelling or bleeding, call your doctor.

2. Discomfort usually is mild after the procedure, but if you have pain you can take acetaminophen (brand name: Tylenol), two 325-mg tablets every 4 hours, or ibuprofen (brand names: Advil, Motrin, Nuprin), three 200-mg tablets three times a day with food.

3. Very rarely, the needle used for the aspiration can penetrate too deeply, allowing air to leak around the lung. You should call your doctor if you develop any shortness of breath or pain when taking a deep breath the day after the procedure.

4. A Band-Aid is placed on the aspiration site after the procedure. The Band-Aid can be removed if it is causing itching, or on the day after the procedure.

5. Your doctor or nurse should call you with the results of the evaluation of the cells removed from your breast. If you have not heard from our office after 2 weeks, please call to get the results.

6. Despite a reassuring result on the evaluation of the cells from the breast, it is still possible that a malignancy (cancer) could be present within the breast. The fine-needle aspiration of the breast is not a perfect test. However, if the physical exam, mammography, and the results of the needle aspiration all suggest that the lump in the breast is benign, there is a greater than 99% chance you do not have a cancer at that site. It is important that you follow-up with your doctor as directed. A repeat mammogram or physical exam may be recommended within the next year.

This handout provides a general overview on this subject and may not apply to everyone. Talk to your family doctor to find out if this information applies to you and to get more information.

INFORMED CONSENT FORM

Fine-Needle Aspiration of the Breast

PATIENT: ______________________________

DATE: ____________________

1. I hereby authorize Dr. ____________________ to perform the procedure known as fine-needle aspiration of the breast.

2. I understand that the procedure is used to evaluate lumps in the breast tissue, and to diagnose cysts and tumors. If the breast lump is a cyst, then the aspiration can drain the cyst and relieve discomfort. I understand that if the lump is a solid tumor, the aspiration may provide cells that will be sent to a laboratory for further analysis. I understand that this aspiration procedure may result in the need for additional procedures. I understand that the practice of medicine is not an exact science, and that no guarantee can be made regarding the outcome of my planned procedure.

3. My doctor has explained to me that this procedure is generally safe, but that certain risks accompany any surgical procedure. Risks associated with the fine needle aspiration of the breast include:

   Bleeding and bruising in the breast tissue

   Pain associated with the needle aspiration or healing process

   Allergic reaction to medications (if used) or surgical instruments

   Pneumothorax—air introduced around the lung from the needle insertion

   Rare infection in the breast tissue

   Rare unusual reactions, including possible death following any surgical procedure

4. I understand that there are alternatives to this procedure, including surgical excision of the lump, no procedure and clinical follow-up, or monitoring alone with radiographic procedures such as mammography or ultrasound. I understand that I can refuse this procedure.

5. I understand that unforeseen conditions may alter the planned procedure. I give permission to my doctor to alter the planned procedure (such as to place a suture to control bleeding) if necessary, or to administer additional anesthetics or other medications if I should need them for the completion of my procedure.

6. I have read this form and other sheets given to me by my physician. I have had my questions answered to my satisfaction.

WITNESS: ______________________________

PATIENT: ______________________________

DATE: ______________________________

MINOR: ______________________________

PARENT: ______________________________

NURSING INSTRUCTIONS

Fine-Needle Aspiration of the Breast

PATIENT PREPARATION

The patient is undressed from the waist up and gowned. The patient is laid supine on the table and the ipsilateral arm (same side as the lump) elevated above the head.

NONSTERILE TRAY FOR THE PROCEDURE

Nonsterile gloves

4 × 4 gauze

Alcohol wipes

2 Euro-Med FNA 21-gauge needles (open one package and have one package unopened as backup if additional aspiration is attempted)

4 glass slides with the patient's name and date written on the frosted end of the slides

Transport container for the slides for transport to the laboratory

Cytofixative spray

Bandage

POSTPROCEDURE NURSING INSTRUCTIONS

Immediately after the aspiration, gauze is placed over the site and the patient or nurse should hold direct pressure for 5 to 10 minutes. A bandage then can be applied to the skin at the aspiration site.

The slides must be accurately marked. The laboratory may dispose of the slides if the patient's name and the date are not recorded. The laboratory request must identify the sample as a breast fine-needle aspiration.

The needle should be disposed of in a proper sharps container. Bloody gauze can be placed in an appropriate biohazard waste container.

PROCEDURE RECORDING FORM

Fine-Needle Aspiration of the Breast

PATIENT NAME: ______________________________

AGE: ______________

DATE: ______________

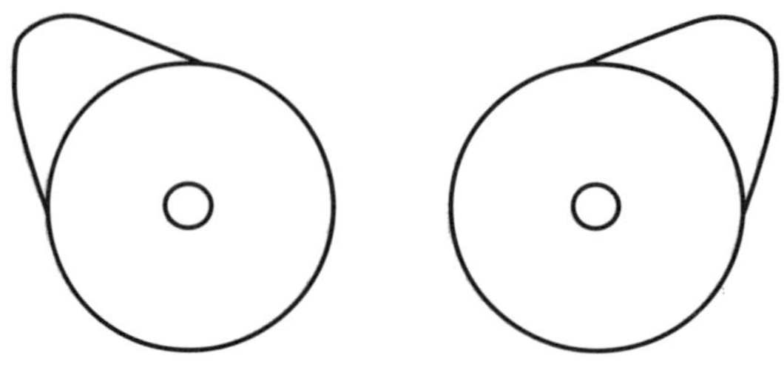

Diameter size of the lesion(s): ______________________________
Date of most recent mammogram: ______________________________
Findings: ______________________________

Circle the Correct Responses:

Pain at the site?	Yes	No
Prior surgical biopsy?	Yes	No
Smooth-walled lesion?	Yes	No
Mass fixed to the chest wall?	Yes	No
Prior needle aspiration at site?	Yes	No
Axillary nodes?	Yes	No
Skin dimpling?	Yes	No
Rock-hard mass?	Yes	No
Prior cysts?	Yes	No
Nipple discharge?	Yes	No

Procedure Description: The patient gave informed consent for the procedure. Other options were discussed, and the patient elected to undergo needle aspiration. The patient lay supine, and the lump was isolated in the fingertips of the physician's nondominant hand. The skin was prepped with alcohol, and a 21-gauge needle was placed within the lesion. A vacuum effect was created by the syringe. The needle tip was moved back and forth within the lesion 10 to 20 times (if no fluid was obtained), and the cellular material was pulled into the needle hub. The needle was withdrawn, and direct pressure was applied to the aspiration site. A bandage was placed. Smears were made and fixed if cellular material was aspirated. The patient tolerated the procedure well.

Bloody fluid obtained?	Yes	No
If yes, sent for evaluation?	Yes	No
Mass palpated after cyst aspiration?	Yes	No
Postprocedure instruction sheet given?	Yes	No

Complications: ______________________________
Impression:
Plan:

Physician: ______________
CC: ______________

CHAPTER 20

Fusiform Excision Procedure

PATIENT INFORMATION

Fusiform Excision Procedure

What is a fusiform excision biopsy?

The fusiform excision technique is a simple way to remove tumors or growths from the skin or tissues below the skin. The term biopsy refers to the removal of tissue for examination under the microscope. This procedure frequently is performed to evaluate whether a growth is cancerous. The fusiform excision is shaped somewhat like a football—longer in length than width.

Why don't you just cut a circle around the tumor to remove it?

Circular cuts remove less skin than the fusiform excision, but a circle doesn't stitch closed very well. A circle will leave elevated skin bunched up at the ends (called dog ears, because the wound looks like the pointed ears on a dog's head). The fusiform excision technique provides a good biopsy specimen and closes in a straight line that usually results in a thin, flat scar.

Are there any complications after this surgery?

Any surgical procedure can result in complications. Bleeding, bruising, or infection can occur in the wound. Despite gentle handling of the skin, the edges of the skin occasionally may die and produce a wider scar. Rarely, damage can occur to structures beneath the skin (such as the nerves or arteries). These problems are very uncommon with this procedure.

Will I feel any pain during this procedure?

Your doctor will numb (anesthetize) the skin under and around the growth before starting the procedure. Every effort will be made to ensure that you will not feel any pain from the procedure. However, you still will have normal feeling in the skin a short distance away from the surgical site. You may feel some tugging of the skin, or even feel the doctor rest his or her hand on the skin during the procedure. In the rare event that you feel sharp pain, tell your doctor right away.

Will stitches be needed to close the wound?

Yes. Sutures (stitches) are required to close the wound created by the procedure. Skin sutures are used to improve the final scar's appearance, and will need to be removed in the days or weeks following the procedure. The timing of skin suture removal varies by body site, and your doctor will tell you when to return. Your doctor may also place absorbable sutures deep inside the wound to control bleeding, but they don't need to be taken out (the body will absorb them).

This handout provides a general overview on this subject and may not apply to everyone. Talk to your family doctor to find out if this information applies to you and to get more information.

PATIENT INSTRUCTIONS

Following Fusiform Excision Procedure

How to care for a sutured incision

1. Your doctor may ask you to apply direct pressure with your hand on the incision site for the first 2 hours following the procedure. If the bandage becomes bloody, you can replace it with dry gauze or a Band-Aid. If the site keeps bleeding, apply direct pressure again for several minutes. This should stop the bleeding. If the wound bleeds heavily, call your doctor's office.

2. You should remove your bandage the day after the procedure. Your doctor may ask you to replace it with a Band-Aid every day for the next few days. Most wounds do not need to be bandaged after that time. However, you may decide to wear a Band-Aid to protect the incision site from rubbing against clothing or to absorb any drainage that might occur.

3. Keep the incision clean and dry for the first 36 hours after the procedure. You should not shower the day of the surgery or the day after the surgery, but you may take a sponge bath. Washing with soap and water is permitted after the second day. Showering is preferred over bathing when you have sutures (stitches) or wound tape covering the incision site. Gently towel dry the incision site after washing.

4. During the healing process, most edges of the incision site become slightly red. Call your doctor's office if the redness increases or extends more than 1/2 inch from the wound. Call your doctor if you have pus from the wound, or if the incision becomes more than mildly tender or painful.

5. Wounds at risk for infection can be washed gently with soap and water each day after the first 36 hours have passed. Your doctor may ask you to put an over-the-counter (available without a prescription) antibiotic ointment (such as Mycitracin) on the incision. Apply the ointment two or four times a day until the stitches are removed.

6. Deep sutures are absorbed by the body and do not need to be removed. Your doctor will remove the sutures that do not absorb. Most skin sutures are taken out in 4 to 21 days, depending on the surgical site. Your doctor will tell you when to return for suture removal.

7. Your doctor may cover the incision site with skin tape (brand name: Steri-Strips) after the sutures are removed. Skin tape provides extra wound support and reduces tension on the healing scar. The skin tape can be removed 3 to 7 days after it is applied, but it sometimes falls off before this.

8. Avoid activities that can cause excessive tension (pulling) on your scar. Your doctor may ask you to avoid lifting, straining, or sports for the first month after your surgery. Call your doctor's office if the incision site pulls apart.

This handout provides a general overview on this subject and may not apply to everyone. Talk to your family doctor to find out if this information applies to you and to get more information.

INFORMED CONSENT FORM

Fusiform Excision Procedure

PATIENT: ______________________________

DATE: ____________________

1. I hereby authorize Dr. ____________________ to perform the procedure known as the fusiform excision biopsy procedure.

2. I understand that this is a procedure performed under local anesthesia to remove a growth or tumor from the skin or the tissues beneath the skin. I understand that this procedure is designed to remove the abnormal tissue for examination under the microscope. It is possible that the growth will not be completely removed, and that another procedure will be required. I understand that the practice of medicine is not an exact science, and that no guarantee can be made regarding the outcome of my planned procedure.

3. My physician has explained to me that this procedure is generally safe, but that certain risks accompany any surgical procedure. Risks associated with the fusiform excision procedure include:

Persistent or excessive bleeding that may require hospitalization or transfusion

Damage to a nerve or artery beneath the surgical site, producing temporary or permanent numbness or muscle weakness

Skin death in the skin to the sides of the surgical wound

Excessive or unsightly scar formation that may require correction at a later date

Allergic reaction to the numbing medication or surgical instruments

Damage to nearby structures, such as the eye or nose when operating on the face

Infection in the local tissues or spreading to other areas

Rare, unusual reactions, including possible death following any surgical procedure.

4. I understand that there are alternatives to this procedure, including shave excision or a partial biopsy technique, such as punch biopsy technique. I understand that I can choose not to biopsy this growth, and I can refuse this procedure.

5. I understand that unforeseen conditions may alter the planned procedure. I give permission to my physician to alter the procedure (such as to suture bleeding vessels at the base of the wound), if necessary, or to administer additional anesthetics or other medications if I should need them for the completion of the procedure.

6. I have read this form and other sheets given to me by my physician. I have had my questions answered to my satisfaction.

WITNESS: ______________________

PATIENT: ______________________

DATE: ______________________

MINOR: ______________________

PARENT: ______________________

NURSING INSTRUCTIONS

Fusiform Excision Procedure

NONSTERILE TRAY FOR ANESTHESIA AND DESIGNING THE FUSIFORM EXCISION

Place the following items on a nonsterile drape covering the Mayo stand:

Nonsterile gloves and mask

Skin marking pen

4 × 4 gauze

Povidone-iodine solution

1 10-mL syringe with a 30-gauge needle attached, filled with 1% lidocaine with epinephrine (Xylocaine with Epinephrine)

STERILE TRAY FOR THE PROCEDURE

Place the following items on a sterile disposable drape covering the Mayo stand:

Sterile gloves

Fenestrated disposable drape

Additional nonfenestrated disposable drape (if desired)

2 sterile bandages to anchor the fenestrated drape

3 hemostats (mosquito clamps)

No. 15 scalpel blade and handle

Needle holder

Mayo or tissue scissors

Iris scissors for cutting sutures

Adson forceps

21-gauge 1 1/2-inch needle (to be bent into a skin hook)

2 inches of 4 × 4 gauze

Suture materials (of the physician's preference)

POSTPROCEDURE NURSING INSTRUCTIONS

The patient or nurse should apply direct pressure to the surgical site with gauze for 10 minutes following the procedure. After this pressure has been applied, the skin can be cleaned with water or sterile saline. The wound can be squeezed to remove any residual blood from beneath the wound.

Antibiotic ointment, 1/2 inch of gauze, and Elastoplast are applied over the clean wound. Tape should be placed around the outer edges of the Elastoplast to keep the edges from curling off the skin. The pressure bandage can be worn until the morning following the procedure.

All instruments should be brushed, washed, rinsed, and dried. The cleaned instruments are then placed in clear sterilization pouches and autoclaved, either individually or as a surgical tray.

Sharps (scalpel blade, needles, suture needles) are disposed of in an appropriate sharps container.

Bloody gauze is disposed of in a biohazard waste container.

The pathology specimen is appropriately labeled and sent for evaluation.

PROCEDURE RECORDING FORM

Fusiform Excision Procedure

PATIENT NAME: ______________________________

DATE: ______________

AGE: ______________

How long has the growth been noted? ______________

Symptoms Associated with the Lesion:

Pain?	Yes	No	Bleeding?	Yes	No
Drainage?	Yes	No	Swelling?	Yes	No
Tenderness?	Yes	No	Irritation?	Yes	No
Itching?	Yes	No	Catches on clothing?	Yes	No

Side affected: Right Left

Diameter of the lesion? ______________

Location of the lesion? ______________________________

Procedure Description: The patient gave informed consent for the procedure. Other options were discussed, and the patient elected to undergo fusiform excision technique. The fusiform excision was drawn with the long axis parallel to the lines of least skin tension. The area was prepped with povidone-iodine solution. The area was anesthetized using the solution circled below, with the solution infiltrated beneath and to the sides of the lesion. The patient tolerated the anesthetic well.

The skin was reprepped with povidone-iodine solution and draped with sterile drapes. The incision was made vertically into the skin using a No. 15 blade. The central fusiform island of skin was grasped in the corner with Adson forceps, and the scalpel blade was used to undermine beneath the lesion in the level of the fat. Once the fusiform island was excised, the tissue was immediately placed in formalin and sent for histologic confirmation. Bleeding from the wound was controlled by applying direct pressure with gauze and placing hemostats onto bleeding vessels. The lateral skin edges were then undermined in the level of the fat using a No. 15 blade. A deep, buried, interrupted, absorbable Vicryl suture was placed down to the level of the fascia to close dead space beneath the wound and provide hemostasis. The skin edge was then everted with placement of interrupted nylon skin sutures.

The patient tolerated the procedure well. Direct wound pressure was applied for 10 minutes following the procedure. The wound was squeezed to remove any residual blood from beneath the wound. The skin was cleaned, antibiotic ointment was applied, and a gauze pressure dressing was applied with Elastoplast. Extensive instructions were given to the patient.

Anesthetic solution: Lidocaine 1% 2% with/without epinephrine

Subcutaneous suture: Vicryl 3-0 4-0 5-0 6-0

Skin suture: Nylon 3-0 4-0 5-0 6-0

Complications: ______________________________

Follow-up for wound check: ______________

Follow-up for suture removal: ______________

Impression:

Plan:

Physician: ______________

CC: ______________

CHAPTER 21

Joint Aspiration and Injection

PATIENT INFORMATION

Joint Aspiration and Injection

What is knee joint aspiration and injection?

Joint aspiration and injection refer to the placement of a needle into a joint cavity to remove fluid for analysis or study, and to inject medicine for pain relief or treatment of a disease (rheumatoid arthritis, gout, pseudogout, infectious arthritis). Sometimes the doctor may only remove fluid from the joint fluid to establish a diagnosis (or cause) for the collection of fluid. In other cases, such as in patients with chronic osteoarthritis, the doctor may only inject medicine to provide pain relief.

How is the procedure performed?

Your doctor will wash the skin over the joint with an antibacterial solution and then select the easiest and safest method of entry into the joint. Although the skin over the joint can be numbed, the injection of the numbing medicine often hurts more than the needle insertion itself. The needle is inserted carefully into the joint, and fluid may be withdrawn. Without having to perform an additional needle-stick, the syringe holding the fluid can be removed, and a syringe containing the medicine is placed onto the needle. The medicine is inserted quickly, and the needle is removed.

Are there risks with needle aspiration and injection?

The risks of this procedure are few. Introducing infection into the joint is very uncommon, occurring in less than 0.01% of patients. Rarely, the needle tip may damage the cartilage surface inside the joint. The greatest risk of injury to the joint appears to be associated with placing too much medicine in the joint, or administering the medicine too often.

Is the procedure painful?

No. Most people find the procedure very tolerable. However, the procedure can hurt if the needle touches the joint surface. Your doctor will try to avoid these surfaces, but sometimes this cannot be prevented. If you feel discomfort, it will generally be very brief. This easy procedure is most commonly performed without an anesthetic (numbing medicine). Pain occurring hours after an injection into a joint can develop from the crystals of medicine that are inserted and may be prevented by taking an anti-inflammatory medicine such as ibuprofen (brand names: Advil, Motrin, Nuprin).

If I had a large amount of fluid removed from the joint, can it come back?

Yes. A collection of fluid within the joint is called an effusion. It is common for an effusion to recur after removal of a large amount of fluid. Some experts recommend that an elastic (ACE) wrap be placed over the joint after removal of large amounts of fluid.

If medicine is injected, how long will it be effective?

The response to medicine injected into the joint is variable. Some people get lasting relief, whereas others may only notice improvement for days to weeks. Call your doctor if the pain returns quickly.

This handout provides a general overview on this subject and may not apply to everyone. Talk to your family doctor to find out if this information applies to you and to get more information.

PATIENT INSTRUCTIONS

Following Joint Aspiration and Injection

1. A bandage was placed over the needle insertion site. You can remove it at any time.

2. One complication of a joint injection is postinjection flare. This is a rare inflammatory reaction to the medicine placed in the joint. The reaction produces intense pain, beginning about 6 to 12 hours after the injection. Patients usually complain that their pain is worse than it was before the injection was performed. To blunt or eliminate this reaction, take ibuprofen (brand names: Advil, Motrin, Nuprin), three 200-mg tablets three times a day, for at least the first 2 days after the injection.

3. If a large amount of fluid was removed from the joint, you may be asked to wear an elastic (ACE) wrap over the site. The wrap is applied to create support and pressure that may reduce the tendency for the fluid to come back. Do not wrap the ACE wrap so tightly that the extremity becomes numb or looks blue.

4. If laboratory studies were performed on the joint fluid, the results should come back in the next few days. Your doctor's office will contact you with the results. Please keep your scheduled follow-up appointment with your doctor.

5. Infection in the joint is very uncommon after joint aspiration and injection. If the joint becomes red, warm, tender, or if you develop a fever in the first few days after the procedure, please call your doctor.

6. If your joint was injected with medicine and local anesthetic, it may be numb for several hours after the procedure. Avoid heavy exercise or placing excessive strain on the injected joint (e.g., carrying children or heavy objects) for the first 2 weeks after the procedure. Jumping up and down, for instance, can place a heavy load on an anesthetized knee and should be avoided.

7. Joint pain may slowly return after an injection. Some people receive long-term pain relief, but for most people the pain gradually returns. Continue your long-term medicine for the joint as prescribed by your doctor.

INFORMED CONSENT FORM

Joint Aspiration and Injection

PATIENT: ______________________________

DATE: ____________________

1. I hereby authorize Dr. ____________________ to perform arthrocentesis or aspiration and injection of a joint. The joint is: ____________________.

2. I understand that this is a procedure performed by placing a needle into the joint. The goal is to withdraw fluid from the joint to provide pain relief, to analyze the fluid under the microscope, and, possibly, to inject medication into the joint for additional relief. I understand that the removal of fluid may be needed to find out why the fluid was present. I understand that fluid may reaccumulate after the removal. I understand that the medication that may be injected is a corticosteroid and may not provide long-lasting relief. I understand that the practice of medicine is not an exact science, and that no guarantee can be made regarding the outcome of my planned procedure.

3. My doctor has explained to me that this procedure generally is safe, but that certain risks accompany any surgical procedure. Risks associated with joint aspiration and injection include:

    Pain associated with the procedure if the needle touches joint surfaces

    Injection into an artery or vein if the needle tip was misplaced

    Damage to a nerve or joint surface from the needle or medication

    Rare introduction of infection into the joint

    Increased joint pain after injection of medication, or the postinjection flare reaction

    Rare, unusual reactions, including possible death following any surgical procedure

4. I understand that there are alternate diagnostic and treatment options to this procedure. I understand that I can refuse this procedure.

5. I understand that unforeseen conditions may alter the planned procedure. I give permission to my doctor to alter the procedure (such as to remove extra fluid for laboratory study), if necessary, or to administer additional anesthetics or other medication if I should need them for the completion of my procedure.

6. I have read this form and other sheets given to me by my physician. I have had my questions answered to my satisfaction.

WITNESS: ____________________

PATIENT: ____________________

DATE: ____________________

MINOR: ____________________

PARENT: ____________________

NURSING INSTRUCTIONS

Joint Aspiration and Injection

PATIENT PREPARATION

The patient is seated comfortably on the examination table. Clothing is removed from over the affected joint. An absorbent pad is placed underneath the affected joint. If the joint is to be injected, the preferred medications are prepared. The anesthetic is always drawn up first, and then the steroid, to prevent contamination of the anesthetic stock bottle.

STERILE TRAY FOR THE PROCEDURE

Place the following items on a sterile sheet covering the Mayo stand:

- Sterile gloves
- Sterile fenestrated drape
- 2 10-mL syringes
- 2 21-gauge 1 1/4-inch needles
- 1 inch of 4 × 4 gauze soaked with povidone-iodine solution
- Hemostat (for stabilizing the needle when exchanging the medication syringe for the aspiration syringe)
- Sterile bandage

POSTPROCEDURE INSTRUCTIONS

The skin is cleansed of any blood or povidone-iodine solution, and the bandage is applied.

Needles are disposed of in an appropriate sharps container.

Soiled or bloodied gauze is disposed of in an appropriate biohazard waste container.

The aspirated joint fluid is labeled and sent for studies as directed by the physician.

Medication bottles are stored in the cabinet.

PROCEDURE RECORDING FORM

Joint Aspiration and Injection

PATIENT NAME: ____________________

DATE: ____________________

AGE: ____________________

REFERRING PHYSICIAN: ____________________

AFFECTED JOINT: ____________________

Circle All That Apply:

Joint pain?	Yes	No	Joint effusion?	Yes	No
Joint prosthesis?	Yes	No	Overlying redness?	Yes	No
Fever or chills?	Yes	No	Bacteremia?	Yes	No
Coagulopathy?	Yes	No	Joint trauma?	Yes	No
Overlying dermatitis?	Yes	No	Prior gout?	Yes	No

Length of time symptoms have been present: ____________________
X-ray findings of the joint: ____________________
Pertinent history: ____________________

Procedure Description: The skin was prepped with povidone-iodine solution. The joint was entered from the ____________ approach using a 21-gauge or ____________ needle. Fluid was obtained for studies. Corticosteroid injection was performed using ____________.
____

Laboratory studies performed:
- ___ Gram stain
- ___ Culture and sensitivity
- ___ CBC count and differential
- ___ Crystal analysis
- ___ Color of the fluid
- ___ AFB and Tb culture
- ___ Glucose, protein, LDH
- ___ Viscosity

Other:

Complications:
Impression:

Plan:

Studies as above.
Postprocedure instruction sheet given to patient.

Physician: ____________________
CC: ____________________

CHAPTER 22

Thoracentesis

PATIENT INFORMATION

Thoracentesis

What is a pleural effusion?

A pleural effusion is the collection of fluid around the lung. If a large amount of fluid is present, the lung can be compressed, which causes difficulty in breathing. The pleural effusion is usually noted on a chest x-ray. The pleural fluid is not normal, and your doctor will probably want to determine why it is there.

How is the fluid in a pleural effusion obtained for analysis?

A small needle is placed between the ribs into the pleural effusion, and fluid is removed for analysis. Placement of the needle into the chest cavity is called thoracentesis. Thoracentesis is done after you have been given a local anesthetic. The procedure generally produces only mild discomfort and can be done in your doctor's office or at the hospital.

Why do I have to get a blood test before thoracentesis?

The evaluation of the fluid in a pleural effusion is greatly enhanced when a blood sample is obtained at the same time. The levels of certain chemicals in the pleural fluid are compared with the amount of the same chemicals in your blood. This information can help your doctor decide on the need for other specific tests that can find the cause of the fluid build-up.

What complications can occur after thoracentesis?

Thoracentesis is relatively safe, but complications can occur. Air leakage from the lung, called pneumothorax, is the most common complication and occurs in 5 to 19% of people who have the test. Most pneumothoraces do not cause problems, but occasionally a tube must be inserted to remove the air. Bleeding, pain, or passing out are all uncommon and occur in less than 1% of individuals.

How long does it take to get the results of the fluid tests?

Your doctor will contact you as soon as the results are available. Your doctor may also order a series of additional tests. It may take a couple of weeks to get all of the information back from the laboratory.

This handout provides a general overview on this subject and may not apply to everyone. Talk to your family doctor to find out if this information applies to you and to get more information.

PATIENT INSTRUCTIONS

Following Thoracentesis

1. You may feel some mild discomfort at the needle injection site. This can usually be controlled by taking ibuprofen (brand names: Advil, Motrin, Nuprin), three 200-mg tablets three times a day with food, or acetaminophen (brand name: Tylenol), two 325-mg tablets every 4 to 6 hours as needed.

2. If you have severe pain, please call your doctor immediately. If you experience difficulty breathing or sharp pain when breathing, please call your doctor.

3. Bleeding can occur at the needle injection site after the procedure. If you develop brisk or continuous bleeding from the site, please call your doctor immediately.

4. Many individuals have a chest x-ray following the procedure. If air is noted to leak from your lung during the procedure, or if you develop difficulty breathing after, then the x-ray can provide your doctor with important information.

5. If your doctor removed a large volume of fluid from your lung to help you breathe, the fluid may come back. If this fluid returns too quickly, you may become short of breath and may need a second procedure.

6. Infection developing from the procedure is very rare, but call your doctor if you develop a fever, cough, or sweating following thoracentesis.

7. Tests will be performed on your blood and pleural fluid. Your doctor's office will notify you of the results once they become available. Occasionally, the initial tests will suggest the need for additional tests to be performed on the fluid that was obtained. The tests may take 2 weeks to complete.

This handout provides a general overview on this subject and may not apply to everyone. Talk to your family doctor to find out if this information applies to you and to get more information.

INFORMED CONSENT FORM

Thoracentesis

PATIENT: ______________________________

DATE: ____________________

1. I hereby authorize Dr. ____________________ to perform the procedure known as thoracentesis.

2. I understand that this is a procedure performed following the administration of local anesthetic to remove fluid from around the lung. I understand that a needle is inserted into my back to remove this abnormal collection of fluid. I understand that testing can be performed on this fluid to evaluate the cause. If a large amount of fluid is present, the removal of the fluid may help my breathing. I understand that the practice of medicine is not an exact science, and that no guarantee can be made regarding the outcome of my planned procedure.

3. My doctor has explained to me that this procedure is generally safe, but that certain risks accompany any surgical procedure. Risks associated with thoracentesis include:

   Bleeding, sometimes requiring transfusion or surgery

   Pain associated with the procedure

   Allergic reaction to the numbing medication or the surgical instruments

   A vasovagal reaction producing nausea or dizziness

   Air leakage from the lung, sometimes requiring placement of a drainage tube

   Needle penetration into the liver or abdomen

   Fluid in the lung if too much fluid is removed from outside the lung

   Rare, unusual reactions, including possible death following any surgical procedure

4. I understand that there are alternatives to this procedure, including surgery, medications, or studies such as CT scans. I understand that these alternatives may not give me some information that can be obtained at thoracentesis. I understand that I can refuse this procedure.

5. I understand that unforeseen conditions may alter the planned procedure. I give permission to alter the procedure (such as to suture closed a bleeding vessel in the skin), if necessary, or to administer additional anesthetics or medications if I should need them for completion of the procedure.

6. I have read this form and other sheets given to me by my physician. I have had my questions answered to my satisfaction.

WITNESS: ______________________

PATIENT: ______________________

DATE: ______________________

MINOR: ______________________

PARENT: ______________________

NURSING INSTRUCTIONS

Thoracentesis

PATIENT PREPARATION

The patient is asked to undress from the waist up.

The patient is seated upright in the middle of the examination table, with the legs off the table to one side. A second adjustable table is raised in front of the patient, with the patient's folded arms resting on the table.

The sterile prepackaged thoracentesis tray is opened and placed on a Mayo stand.

Supplemental sterile gloves are provided, and povidone-iodine solution is poured onto the tray into one of the plastic wells. A sterile hemostat can be added to the tray, if desired.

STERILE THORACENTESIS TRAY

Catheter 18-cm (7-inch) long with a 14-gauge 5.1-cm (2-inch) long needle
Catheter guard
60-mL lock tip syringe
25-gauge 1.6 cm (5/8 inch) needle
22-gauge 5.1 cm (2 inch) needle
3 way stopcock
5-mL syringe
Drainage tube and bag
3 prelabeled 10-mL specimen tubes with caps
2 swab sticks
3 gauze 3 × 3 inch sponges
Puncture site bandage
Fenestrated drape with adhesive strips, and a towel
5 mL of lidocaine HCL (Xylocaine) 1%

POSTPROCEDURE NURSING INSTRUCTIONS

The patient's back can be wiped clear of any remaining povidone-iodine solution.

The bandage is applied over the puncture site.

Disposable needles are disposed of in the appropriate sharps container.

The hemostat should be washed, and resterilized in the autoclave.

Bloody gauze should be disposed of in a biohazard waste container.

The specimen containers should be properly labeled, and laboratory testing paperwork should be completed.

PROCEDURE RECORDING FORM

Thoracentesis

PATIENT NAME: ______________________________

DATE: ______________

AGE: ______________

PLEURAL EFFUSION FIRST NOTED: ______________

PREPROCEDURE CXR: AVAILABLE FOR THE PROCEDURE? Yes No

Greater than 1 cm of fluid layering on the lateral decubitus film? Yes No
Preprocedure bloodwork: Total protein, Glucose, LDH Yes No
Other bloodwork results: ______________

Circle the Correct Responses:

Anticoagulation therapy?	Yes	No	Uncooperative patient?	Yes	No
Patient on mechanical ventilation?	Yes	No	Bleeding disorder?	Yes	No
Active chest wall infection?	Yes	No	Patient with COPD?	Yes	No
Presence of only one lung?	Yes	No	Presence of CHF?	Yes	No
Presence of thrombocytopenia?	Yes	No	Presence of uremia?	Yes	No
Prior thoracic radiation therapy?	Yes	No	Cirrhosis of the liver?	Yes	No
History of prior malignancy	Yes	No	Nephrotic syndrome?	Yes	No
History of tuberculosis?	Yes	No	Recent pancreatitis?	Yes	No

Procedure Description: The patient gave informed consent for the procedure. The patient was seated with the legs off the side of the table and folded arms resting on a table in front of the patient. The level of effusion was determined by percussion, and the needle insertion site was selected one intercostal space below the edge of the effusion. The needle insertion site was marked by indenting the skin with the examiner's fingernail. The sterile tray was opened, and sterile gloves were applied. The skin was cleansed with povidone-iodine solution, and the sterile fenestrated drape was centered over the insertion site. The skin and tissues were anesthetized, with the needle inserted to the upper edge of the rib, and then a Z-track was created with the needle placed into the pleural space. Anesthetic was administered up to the pleural surface. The depth needed to reach the pleura was noted, and the needle was withdrawn. The thoracentesis needle was placed into the anesthetized skin, and a Z-track was created into the pleural space. The catheter was threaded in the needle, and the needle guard was applied. At least 50 mL of fluid were obtained for study. The catheter was withdrawn, skin was cleansed, and a bandage was applied. The patient tolerated the procedure well. The patient was given postprocedure instructions.

Procedure performed on Right Left
Air aspirated during procedure? Yes No
Total fluid removed during the procedure: ______________
Complications: ______________________________
Fluid color: ______________ Fluid characteristics: ______________
Laboratory studies: Routine (WBC with diff., LDH, Glucose, Protein) Yes No
Circle other studies ordered:
KOH Gram stain AFB smear Bacterial culture Tb culture Fungal culture
Cytology Lipid studies LE prep Amylase Rheumatoid factor pH
Impression:

Plan:

Physician: ______________
CC: ______________